THE ESSENTIAL NATURE OF
NEW TESTAMENT PREACHING

The
Essential Nature of
New Testament
Preaching

by

ROBERT H. MOUNCE

ASSOCIATE PROFESSOR AND CHAIRMAN
OF THE DEPARTMENT OF CHRISTIANITY
BETHEL COLLEGE

Wipf & Stock
PUBLISHERS
Eugene, Oregon

Wipf and Stock Publishers
199 W 8th Ave, Suite 3
Eugene, OR 97401

The Essential Nature of New Testament Preaching
By Mounce, Robert H.
Copyright©1960 by Mounce, Robert H.
ISBN: 1-59752-371-2
Previously published by Wm. B. Eerdmans Publishing Company, 1960

To my wife

JEAN

who first commented that the
supreme task of the preacher was
"to lead people into the presence of God."

FOREWORD

This book concerns the *kerygma* — the preached Gospel which the first heralds of Christ proclaimed to the great pagan world of their day, that Gospel which, after nineteen centuries, remains *the* Word from the Beyond for our human predicament. It tells what that Proclamation really was, and how it runs, like a golden thread, through the whole New Testament.

But (someone may say) did not C. H. Dodd say all that was to be said about this in his *Apostolic Preaching?* Dr. Mounce avows his debt to Dr. Dodd, but he does not believe Dodd has said the last word on the subject. He believes, for example, that Dr. Dodd drew too sharp a line between *kerygma* and *didache.* He believes that in his conception of the earliest *kerygma* Dodd laid too much stress on the dawn of the New Age and not enough on God's redemptive activity in Christ. He believes that the *kerygma* developed not from the crudely apocalyptic to the refined and mystical (as in St. John), but rather, under stress of practical requirements, in the direction of the theological and ethical. These are good discussion points; and whether you agree with Dr. Mounce in all of them, you must concede that he argues them well. Moreover, at this point and that, as it seems to me — for example, in his rooting of the *kerygma* in the teaching of Jesus, in his disentangling of pre-Pauline elements from Paul's letters — he breaks fresh ground.

If this sounds rather learned, the fault is mine. There is nothing dull about Dr. Mounce's lucid and *ligato* style or about the sincerity of his Christian conviction. And in his closing chapter he brings his whole work to the crucial test of relevance. He asks: What has true Christian preaching ever been, and what should it always be? And he answers: "The medium through which God contemporizes His historic self-disclosure in Christ, and offers man the opportunity to respond in faith." This is an answer on which P. T. Forsyth,

5

H. H. Farmer, John Knox, J. S. Stewart, and many of us would agree.

Here then is much good matter, well-argued and well-written. May it command many readers!

A. M. Hunter

King's College, Aberdeen

PREFACE

It was far more than mere intellectual curiosity that gave rise to the present investigation. The basic motivation was a deep-seated conviction that the man in the pulpit occupies a position of unrivaled significance in the life and destiny of his fellow man. Standing at the crossroads of time and eternity, he has the exalted privilege to prolong in time that mighty redemptive act of God which in one sense belongs to a specific date in the Roman Imperial Age. As he speaks, somehow his words become the Divine Word. He has mediated the presence of God, and to those who respond in faith the Divine Self-disclosure has become an actuality. It is by way of the pulpit that the cycle of revelation is made complete.

The sacramental nature of preaching is one of the most fruitful advances of contemporary Biblical thought. A closely related discussion, which is far-reaching in its implications, is that of the relation between the Christ of the *kerygma* and the historical Jesus. For Bultmann — whose name is inseparably involved in every facet of the debate — the only thing that can be known for sure about the historical Jesus is that He was an eschatological prophet with a demand for existential decision. Recent studies by "kerygmatic theologians" have tended to temper this position. The very fact that the *kerygma* (regarded as the essential ground of faith) centers in Jesus Christ compels the exploration of what must be an essential relationship between the *kerygma* and the historical Jesus.

Thus the *kerygma* — the message proclaimed by the earliest Christians — is pivotal. But what exactly is the *kerygma?* What was the central thrust of the earliest preaching? And, for that matter, what is the nature of *heralding* in the New Testament — that activity which produced the *kerygma?* While these questions have been answered in part, there is much room for further investigation. The clearer our understanding of the primitive proclamation, the closer we will be to the heart of the Christian faith. The aim of this book is to set

forth the mission and message of the New Testament herald
in such a way as to establish a new perspective into the life
and thought of primitive Christianity.

In the quest for a better understanding of the apostolic
preaching I am indebted to a whole host of Biblical scholars
who, in one way or another, have already investigated some
aspect of the problem. The names of Dodd, Taylor, Jeremias,
Manson, and Hunter — not to mention others almost equally
helpful — will recur throughout the following pages.

I would like to express my appreciation for the friendship
and guidance of Professor A. M. Hunter, D.Phil., Master of
Christ's College, Aberdeen, who has given unstintingly of his
time and the privacy of his study. My thanks are also due
to the librarians of Christ's College and King's College, Aberdeen, for their cheerful assistance, and to my colleague at
Bethel College, the Rev. C. Weintz, who has taken time from
a busy schedule to read the proof sheets.

—ROBERT MOUNCE

CONTENTS

Chapter One

CULTURAL AND LINGUISTIC BACKGROUNDS

WHEN a member of the church at Corinth read that it pleased God through the folly of the *kerygma* to save those who believe, what was the mental image created by this word? Or, what association of ideas was conjured up in his mind by the mention of Jesus' "heralding" of the Kingdom of God?

To give a precise answer to questions like these is no easy matter, for language is a living thing. With the passage of time concepts change and give new meaning to their written symbols. At the same time words shift in their usage and new shades of meaning are read into old ideas. Social, philosophical, and political change all join the movement to keep language in a state of flux. Internal forces, such as the leveling out of metaphors and the trend towards versatility at the expense of precision, complicate understanding and seemingly baffle any exactness in the reproduction of ancient thought. In the case of Greek the problem is particularly acute, for no other language has been less static. From Homer until the present day it has been involved in a process of rapid and continual change.

There was a time when it was generally assumed that the language of the New Testament differed only slightly from classical Greek. Within the last half century, however, historical and archaeological research has produced a vast body of contemporary inscriptions, records, and letters which have shown that the Greek of the New Testament, far from being "the language of the Holy Ghost" (as one pious German scholar put it), is rather the language of the common man — the colloquial idiom of human experience. Many have considered this advance to be the key which at long last has unlocked the door to New Testament thought.

11

Over against this opinion there are those who continue to lay great stress on the Hebraic quality of New Testament Greek. They recognize full well the problem of the New Testament writers in transmitting a mode of thought and a religious vocabulary distinctly Semitic into the language and culture of Hellenism.

How then should we approach the problem of understanding as accurately as possible the concept of heralding as it occurs in the New Testament? The most satisfactory procedure will be first to survey the related terms as they appear in classical Greek. This is basic from a philological standpoint. Then we will turn to the Septuagint to determine the role of the herald in the life and culture of the Old Testament world. Finally — and this is of crucial importance — we will deal with the concept as it occurs in the New Testament itself. While backgrounds are both necessary and helpful, the exact nuance of thought of any New Testament term must ultimately be derived from its specifically Christian associations. Here we are dealing with material written under the impetus of the recognition that God in Christ Jesus has acted in history for the redemption of mankind. The invasion of time by eternity immeasurably heightens and remolds every term employed in an attempt to describe it.

THE ROLE OF THE HERALD IN THE ANCIENT WORLD

In the world of Homer the herald was a man of dignity and held a notable position in the royal court. Men praised him for his intelligence and prudence. As a sign of his regal office he carried a scepter in his hand. While he at times performed certain menial tasks, such as mixing the wine, serving guests, and preparing his master's bath, he was not a slave. He was a freeman whose relationship to his master was that of a comrade or close friend.

The passage of time altered but slightly the role of the herald. The only significant change in the post-Homeric era was that the herald served the state rather than the king. Occasionally it appears that the public viewed certain heralds with considerable suspicion. Official respect, however, was somewhat better. Records show that heralds were usually members of the best social circles and not infrequently honored for outstanding service. In Roman times the herald of the Areopagus acted as president of that body and was responsible for all its resolutions.

The one basic qualification of the herald was that he have a loud, clear, well articulated voice.[1] A primary duty was to make all public proclamations. Like the town crier of recent history, the ancient herald would walk through the streets (usually accompanied by a flock of small children) and call out notices of public interest. At times he used a trumpet to attract the people, but only when necessary, for this was somewhat of an insult to his ability. It also fell to the herald to maintain quiet and order in the public meeting — no job for a timid voice. In the courtroom, where excitement could rise like the crest of a mighty wave, it was his duty to subdue it before it would crash over the heads of the officials.

An interesting, if not amusing, observation is that in the great Hellenic festivals, the heralds would take part in a contest of lung power and enunciation. The victor would then have the privilege of announcing the winners in the other games.

A second qualification for the herald was that he be dignified and possess a reliable character. As may well be imagined, the herald's peculiar temptation lay in the area of talkativeness and exaggeration. Thus it was essential that the herald be a man of considerable self-control. The proclamation must be delivered exactly as it was received. As the mouthpiece of his master he dare not add his own interpretation.

Since for the Greeks there was no separation between religion and politics, it follows that a religious significance would inevitably be attached to the herald. In a foreign land he was considered as under the protection of the gods. An

---

1 This basic qualification has carried through from ancient times until today. A recent obituary to Sir Gerald Wollaston, former Garter King-of-Arms, reads, "Sir Gerald had a fine resonant voice admirably fitted for the reading of royal proclamations" (*The Manchester Guardian*, March 5, 1957, p. 4).

offense against him, even if he should bring an unfriendly report, was irreverence towards the gods and would bring down their wrath. At home the herald played a prominent role in all state religious functions. At the opening of the public assembly he would command silence and pray for the welfare of the city. His most prominent religious function was in connection with the great cultic sacrifices. Along with the priest, the herald would select the sacrificial animal, help in the elaborate preparations, and actually partake in the sacrificial meal. As a token of honor he would receive the tongue of the slain animal.

Certain of the heralds were held to have been appointed by the gods as special envoys. One such herald was the Stoic philosopher. Since philosophy and religion had merged into one, the philosopher's message became an exposition of divine secrets revealed by the gods. Leaving home and country, he wandered through the land with knapsack and staff as his only conveniences. Strong in his convictions, he fearlessly preached a stern message of ascetic discipline and promised a felicity higher than even the emperor could offer. In spite of his similarity to the early Christian missionary (cf. Matt. 10:5-15) there was one basic difference. The Stoic proclaimed his message on the basis of his observation of men, while the Christian was driven to speak by the invasion of God into the affairs of man in the person of Jesus Christ His Son.

In summary we may say that the herald was a figure of prominence and importance in the Hellenistic world. His employer was the king or the state; his duty was to make official proclamations; and because of his vital role in cultic sacrifice, he acquired a distinct religious significance.

HERALDING IN THE SEPTUAGINT

When we turn to the Septuagint we find that the noun κῆρυξ (herald), which appeared so often in Hellenistic literature, occupies a much less conspicuous place. In fact, of its four occurrences (Gen. 41:43, Dan. 3:4, Sir. 20:15, and IV Mac. 6:4) two are non-canonical, one is used in a foreign setting, and the other has no Hebrew equivalent. Likewise

the related noun   κήρυγμα (the message proclaimed) is sel-
dom used.

With the verb, however, the picture changes: κηρύσσειν
(to proclaim — transliterated *kerussein*) occurs more than
thirty times. A quick survey of *kerussein* in the Septuagint
shows that in every instance it originates with a person of
authority. This person may be a foreign potentate (such as
Pharaoh, Cyrus, or Nebuchadnezzar), a leader of Israel (as
Aaron or Moses), or God Himself through the prophets. Since
this somewhat external classification corresponds to a more
basic division inherent in the concept itself, it may be conveniently used as a framework for the discussion of heralding
in the Old Testament.

(1) *Proclamations by foreign kings*

It is in this first group that we would expect to see the
strongest reflection of Hellenistic usage. And that is so. In
Daniel 3, when Nebuchadnezzar's golden image had been
completed and an impressive group of Babylonian notables
had gathered for the occasion, the instructions on how to do
proper obeisance were proclaimed by "the heralds" (v. 4).
Such a scene would not have been at all strange in Homer.
Making official proclamation for the king, especially when it
had a cultic tinge, most naturally fell to the herald.

Another characteristic activity of the Hellenistic herald was
to go before a royal personage and call out his approach.
This, too, finds expression in the Septuagint. After Joseph
had interpreted Pharaoh's dream and advised him how to
cope with the approaching famine, he was dressed in the gar-
ments of nobility mounted upon a horse, and "a herald made
proclamation before him" (Gen. 41:43). Similar is the case
of Haman and Mordecai (Esther 6:9-11). The wily Haman,
confident that he was engineering his own exaltation, insisted
that it should be "one of the king's most noble princes" who
would dress him in royal robes and "make proclamation" before him as he rode through the city. How ironic that Haman
himself had to play the part of the herald — and that for a
bitter enemy.

It is probable that Cyrus' proclamation concerning the rebuilding of the temple was spread throughout the captivity by means of heralds (II Chron. 36:22). It is also reasonable to posit a herald in the official proclamation of Daniel as the third ruler of Babylon (Dan. 5:29, Theodotion), as well as in the announcement of the penitential fast proclaimed by the King of Nineveh (Jonah 3:7-9). Thus, both by direct statement and reasonable inference, the Septuagint bears witness to the role of the herald in foreign courts.

(2) Proclamation by those governing Israel

The second group of passages is connected with the governing of Israel by various leaders. While Judaism had no specific office of herald as such, the activity of heralding is everywhere seen. When Hezekiah and his assembly established a decree that a "proclamation" should go out in all Israel (II Chron. 30:5-10), the letters were taken by couriers and the contents announced by them. While these couriers were not officially designated as heralds, they were a distinct group whose activity was virtually the same as that of the Greek herald. The fast which Jehoshaphat proclaimed in "all Judah" would of necessity have to be implemented by some such group (II Chron. 20:3; cf. II Kings 10:20). If the instructions of Moses to cease bringing offerings for the sanctuary (Exod. 36:6), or those of Joash to start bringing in the temple tax (II Chron. 24:9) had originated in Athens, the public proclamation would most certainly have been handled by the royal herald.

It should be noticed that the heralding which originated with the leaders of Israel was closely related to cultic worship. After repairing and purifying the house of the Lord, Hezekiah sent a proclamation throughout all Israel that the people should come to Jerusalem to keep the Passover (II Chron. 28:1ff.).[2] The fast proclaimed by Jehoshaphat in view of the approaching armies of the Moabites and Ammonites (II Chron. 20:3) was religious, although occasioned by im-

2 A similar case is Esdras' proclamation in all Jewry that the people should gather at Jerusalem, there to mourn for their great iniquity and to put away their strange wives (I Esd. 9:3).

pending calamity. Jehu's "great sacrifice" and "solemn festival" that he proclaimed to the followers of Baal (II Kings 10:20) was cultic, as was Aaron's idolatrous proclamation of a "feast to the Lord" (Exod. 32:5). If the occurrences of *kerussein* in the Septuagint have given us a fair cross section of heralding in Judaism, we may say that it always has a definite relationship to some phase of the cult.

In this second group of passages heralding has taken on a new note — the note of urgency. When foreign kings bestowed honor, although the occasion was deemed important, there was no real urgency involved — no do-or-die quality. Back of Israel's heralding, however, was a compulsion that lent the situation an air of extreme urgency. While its causes were sometimes external (such as Jehoshaphat's fear of the invading armies), more often it arose from within. Hezekiah's reform, for instance, was the result of an abhorrence of the idolatry that had corrupted the land.

Kerussein, as it is used in the Wisdom Literature, is also fraught with this same sense of urgency. Since Wisdom has a message of vital importance, man must hear or perish in his folly. Thus she goes wherever men may congregate — in the public square (Prov. 1:20), at the city gates (1:21), or at the crossroads (8:2) — and there she makes her proclamation. Finding a strategic place "on the top of the walls" (1:21), or "on lofty eminences" (8:2), she urgently sends forth her message.

(3) *Proclamation through the prophets*

When we turn to the prophets we find that the verb *kerussein* is, in the majority of instances, used in connection with some national emergency. In Joel the locusts have for several consecutive years swept in and caused unprecedented devastation. Lack of rain has made a bad situation even worse. For Joel these are signs of the approaching day of the Lord. Hence he urges his countrymen to sanctify a fast and proclaim a solemn assembly (1:14, 2:15). Perhaps Yahweh will be moved by national contrition to grant them help. Impending disaster is also the setting in Hosea. Israel has been defiled by leaders who know not Yahweh, and punishment is on its way. Hence the prophet calls for alarm signals to be sounded on the high watchtowers and "proclamation" to be made (5:8).

Kerussein is also used — and this is peculiar to the prophets — of joyful shouting. In Zephaniah 3:14 the daughter of Jerusalem (a personification of the people) is told to "rejoice . . . cry out [*kerusse*] . . . delight thyself with all thy heart." The Lord has taken away thy iniquities: therefore "proclaim" with joy and exultation. In Zechariah 9:9 the motive for joyful proclamation is the approach of the Messianic King.

Finally, *kerussein* is used in Isaiah to portray the activity of the Servant of the Lord (Isa. 61:1). Here we find the proper transition between the Old and New Testaments, for Jesus maintained that His ministry was the fulfillment of this prophetic portion (Luke 4:21). Sent by God and anointed by the Spirit, He was to "proclaim liberty to the captives and recovery of sight to the blind." Herein lies a uniqueness that characterizes New Testament heralding: while it proclaims, it brings to pass its proclamation. The proclamation of liberty at the same time frees. The preaching of sight opens blind eyes.

The various uses of *kerussein* in the prophets have in common a sense of urgency. And whether this urgency arises from a national emergency or the supreme importance of the Messianic ministry, it makes the message vibrantly alive. At the same time there is an important development. A new note of joy comes to the front. On the lips of the "daughter of Jerusalem" it begins to have Messianic overtones. In Isaiah it is connected with the glad tidings heralded by the Servant and the prophetic realization of the Messianic age.

Thus the way is prepared for the supreme proclamation of time and eternity, that "God was in Christ, reconciling the world unto himself." *Kerussein* passes from the secular to the sacred. It correspondingly attains a new sense of urgency. This urgency becomes permeated with Messianic joy. What cluster of terms can be better suited to portray the public proclamation of the Kingdom of God!

Chapter Two

JOHN THE BAPTIST: MESSIANIC HERALD

AFTER four hundred years without prophetic testimony, the silence of the Judean wilderness was shattered by the proclamation, "Repent, for the kingdom of heaven is at hand" (Matt. 3:2). Dressed in the garb of the prophet Elijah, John the Baptist had arrived to prepare a nation for the coming of the "mightier one." His task had two aspects: negatively, "to destroy the confidence that the Messianic hope was a gilt-edged security from which every reasonably good Jew might expect to draw a dividend,"[1] and positively, to create a New Israel. The former was necessary because the Jews had come to take it for granted that proper heredity insured entrance to the coming Messianic era. John spoke out in no uncertain terms against this cherished tradition. He insisted that entrance to the Kingdom demanded nothing less than "a fundamental revolution in moral purpose." In a sense, he excommunicated an entire nation and restored the people only when they gave evidence of genuine sorrow for sin.

This act of repentance was then to be symbolized by the rite of baptism. John's baptism, similar to, and probably stemming from, proselyte baptism, differed in its demand for a genuine change of heart. Hardly a sacrament "operating magically and ritualistically to wash away sinful matter,"[2] it is better understood as "an extension of the symbolic actions of the prophets."[3] It was a baptism unto (εἰς) the forgiveness of sins, viz., forgiveness was the ultimate result for which the rite was preparatory. To submit to it was to admit

1 T. W. Manson, *The Servant-Messiah*, p. 47.

2 As Otto (*The Kingdom of God and the Son of Man*, p. 77) maintains.

3 W. F. Flemington, *The New Testament Doctrine of Baptism*, p. 22. The extension lay in that it was not the isolated act of a prophet, but a corporate act in which all should share.

19

the inadequacy of Abrahamic descent. It was a solemn indication of moral renovation.

The question to be asked here is, In what sense was John a herald? What exactly did he proclaim? In both Mark 1:4 and Luke 3:3, John is said to have proclaimed a "baptism of repentance for the forgiveness of sins." The parallel in Matthew 3:2 summarizes John's preaching in direct address: "Repent, for the kingdom of heaven is at hand."[4] In Acts 10:37, Peter refers to the "baptism that John proclaimed," and Paul defines it further as a "baptism of repentance" (Acts 13:24). *Kerussein* is used but once in connection with the coming One (Mark 1:7).

What demands our attention is that the content of John's proclamation is not, as we might have supposed, an eschatological event but, rather, an ethical demand. It is true that he speaks much of the "mightier one" who will come in power and judgment, but this is not the primary content of his message. It forms, rather, the eschatological sanction for the ethical summons. Here the *kerygma* is the moral demand. The crucial element is "do something" — the "because of something" is only the motive for action. This understanding of John's *kerygma* is in harmony with his total ministry. As forerunner, he did not merely announce the coming of the "mightier one," but he was deeply involved in the preparation of the people's hearts.

4 F. C. Burkitt (*Christian Beginnings*, pp. 15-16) says that the phrase "the kingdom is at hand" is the result of a Matthaean assimilation of the message of John with that of Jesus (Matt. 4:17), and that the message of John was a single word — Repent. However, as the entire concept of a coming one, judgment, etc., is totally eschatological, the enunciation of the motive for repentance is most reasonable. Duncan (*Jesus, Son of Man*, p. 78) writes, "There can be no effective ethical preaching divorced from eschatology." A predisposition to see in John little more than a "prophet of doom," and to overlook the evidence of the context, seems to be the conditioning factor of the omission. Otto's use of "the law and the prophets were until John" to prove that John could have brought no message of the Kingdom of heaven (*op. cit.*, p. 69) overlooks the fact that "all the prophets who have spoken, from Samuel and those who came afterwards, also proclaimed these days" (Acts 3:24). Why could not have John the Baptist?

The two elements in Matthew's summary (3:2) — ethical and eschatological — are expanded in turn in verses 7-10 and 11-12. Those who come with unrepentant hearts are stopped short. Only the bearing of the appropriate fruits of repentance can stay the hand that wields the axe of judgment. Abrahamic lineage is worthless. The imminence of the Kingdom is seen in the coming of a "mightier one" who will gather His wheat but burn the chaff. Mark's account lacks any direct reference to eschatological judgment. Luke (3:7-18) includes all the Matthaean expansion plus five additional verses (10-14) in which John interprets his repentance command to those asking, "What shall we do?" The imperfect tense in Luke 3:7 indicates that what follows is the general burden of John's preaching. Even a casual glance at these verses will show that John's message was predominantly ethical. Writing against the position that "according to Mark and Q, the mission of John was fundamentally eschatological,"[5] Burkitt concludes, "As I understand it, the teaching of John was wholly ethical."[6] In this we concur, but quickly add that ethics are meaningless except against an eschatological background.

Any view of the preaching of John is necessarily conditioned by one's total understanding of the man and his mission. At this point the Baptist often suffers from unjust caricaturization as a pessimistic prophet of doom — an ascetic with a "gloomy fearful disposition"[7] — a preacher with no message of deliverance or hope, but only of stern warning and violent retribution.

To be sure, the wrath of God played a prominent role in John's religious understanding. With vivid metaphor and unashamed fervor he proclaimed the righteous reprisal of divine holiness. His conviction played no favorites and spared no man. The religious rulers were denounced for their serpentine nature. Even Herod was rebuked for his moral laxity.

However, to let this more dramatic side of John blind us to the rest of the man is to create an imaginary person who is only

5 Foakes-Jackson and Kirsopp Lake, *The Beginnings of Christianity*, I, 103.

6 Burkitt, *op. cit.*, p. 77.

7 Otto, *op. cit.*, p. 77.

superficially related to the Baptist. John's message of repentance must be seen as a part of the total program of the coming
Kingdom. It was not an end in itself. His ministry must be
labeled, Part I: Preparation (more to follow). It was "the
first stage of the bringing in of the Kingdom."[8] It fell to John
to carry out that part of the total message which was of necessity more stern. But this is something quite different from
seeing him as only a gloomy pessimist. It was not an obsession with the distasteful that determined the tone of his message;
it was the message itself that was stern. The necessity of repentance laid hold of him as an instrument for propagation
and he simply passed it on. We should not blame the execu-
tioner for the decision of the State. But further, does not repentance itself issue in Kingdom felicity? Can the joys of the
coming Kingdom be inherited apart from genuine sorrow for
past complicity with the King's enemies? No, the two are inseparably linked. Over the door to the Kingdom it is written,
"God opposes the proud, but gives grace to the humble" (I Pet.
5:5).

Further, it should be noticed that John's sternness is reserved
for those who come without repentant hearts. To all he says,
Repent, but the vivid picture of unquenchable fire is reserved
for those who trespass in insincerity. Luke's general summary
of John's teaching (3:7-18) is clearly divided in Matthew, and
the epithet "brood of vipers," as well as what follows, is directed
to the Pharisees and Sadducees (3:7). All repentance has an
eschatological background, but as a wise prophet and the Messianic forerunner, John reserved the more vivid colors and the
bolder strokes for those who would trifle with the divine
demand.

But even a message of repentance may be permeated with
glimpses of coming joy — indications that although repentance
is the immediate task, something better lies beyond. One such
indication is that the long-awaited Kingdom is now at hand.
The "mightier one" whose justice demands that He burn the
chaff, will also in love gather the wheat. Is this not a joyful
prospect? John also boldly declares that the coming One will

8 S. H. Hooke, *The Kingdom of God in the Experience of Jesus*, p. 23.

baptize men with the Holy Spirit[9] — long considered as a vital part of the Messianic blessedness.

Luke, after speaking of fiery judgment on the unrepentant, goes on to say, "So, with many other exhortations" — that is, of a different kind[10] — "he preached good news (εὐηγγελίζετο)" (3:18). Thus, John's message was not always as invective as the preceding pericope might suggest. He also used exhortations "of a different kind." And especially, he preached *good news*. Is it possible that we have here only a gloomy pessimist with a repentant cast of mind? Or would it be more correct to say that he is a fearless messenger, appointed by God to the solemn task of preparation, and adapting his message to fit his particular audience?[11]

For that matter, is not the very title, "prophet of doom,"

9 It is often held that the original version in Q was "baptize with fire," and this came to be interpreted by the early Church as the baptism of the Holy Spirit. Thus, in Matthew and Luke we have both the original saying plus the interpretation (cf. T. W. Manson, *The Sayings of Jesus*, pp. 40-41). I am reluctant to accept such a reconstruction because while reference to "fire" occurs along with baptism by the Holy Spirit in Matthew and Luke, reference to baptism by the Spirit is found in all four Gospels. It is also found on the lips of the Lord in Acts 1:5, and Peter refers back to it in Acts 11:16 when explaining what happened in his dealings with Cornelius. The passing reference to the ignorance of a remote group of John's disciples some twenty years later (Acts 19:1-6) does not seem to supply sufficient reason for such a thorough revision. Especially when this group may well have been a segment of those who had come to think of John as the Messiah, and would naturally oppose reference to one with a superior baptism. Cullmann (*The Early Church*, pp. 177-78) cites evidence for such a group and concludes that the opening of the Fourth Gospel is a polemic against them. Duncan (*op. cit.*, p. 81n.), commenting on the above reconstruction, says, "Such a suggestion perhaps owes some of its plausibility to a desire to connect John's message solely with judgment."

10 The Greek is ἕτερα not ἀλλά.

11 It is interesting that in Josephus' portrait of John (*Antiquities*, xviii. 5. 2) he is pictured as an ethical reformer. Eschatological judgment is not to be found. He also says that the people were "highly elated" at hearing John's words — not a natural reaction to a gloomy message. This telltale phrase is not unlike Jesus' reminder to the people that they "were willing to *rejoice* for a while in his [John's] light" (John 5:35).

somewhat of a misnomer? Every great prophet must have an
element of judgment in his message. Of course, if that is all
he has, he cannot be called a true prophet in the Biblical
sense. Side by side with the denunciations of Amos are prom-
ises of deliverance. Joel, who cries out against the wickedness
of the land, can also promise that the Lord will again dwell
in Zion (cf. 1:15, 3:16). Judgment must always be part of
the message of the prophet who recognizes that man may refuse God's mercy. But it is hardly fair to say that this makes
him a "prophet of doom."

The tendency to glorify Jesus' "positive message" at the expense of John's "gloomy outbursts" grows from a desire to
contrast the two messages. Very often such neat contrasts
can only be achieved at the expense of glossing over unfavorable material. Did Jesus, in fact, always proclaim such a
"positive" message? When confronted with studied opposition, the "gentle Nazarene" did not hesitate to denounce the
Pharisees in terms fully as severe as John had employed.
"You serpents, you brood of vipers,[12] how are you to escape
being sentenced to hell?" (Matt. 23:33). He speaks of "unquenchable fire" (Mark 9:43) and "outer darkness" (Matt. 25:
30) — a place of "eternal punishment" (Matt. 25:46) where
"men will weep and gnash their teeth" (Matt. 13:42; cf. also
Luke 13:28). He says that He "came to cast fire upon the
earth" (Luke 12:49), and that "unless you repent you will
all likewise perish" (Luke 13:5). How then can the two
ministries be contrasted in such an absolute fashion?[13] We
would not maintain that they are qualitatively the same, but
only that they are not absolutely opposed. They are comple-
mentary, not antithetical.

If John were only a fanatic, morbidly occupied with thoughts
of impending doom, it would be difficult to understand Jesus'
verdict that "among those born of women there has risen no
one greater than John the Baptist" (Matt. 11:11, Luke 7:28),

12 This striking epithet may well have been borrowed from John.
Cf. Matt. 3:7 and Luke 3:7.
13 Cf. Otto's chapter on "The Contrast between the Person and Message of Jesus and the Person and Message of John" (op. cit., pp. 76-81),
which is but "a mere outline" (p. 75).

or His reference to John as a "burning and shining lamp" who brought rejoicing to the multitudes (John 5:35). It is also very doubtful whether a thoroughgoing pessimist could have so moved a nation that even after his death the religious leaders were afraid because of public opinion to claim a human origin for John's message — and that at the price of considerable embarrassment (Mark 11:27-33 and parallels). John's ministry had made such a mark on Herod that on hearing of the fame of Jesus he identified Him as John *redivivus* (Matt. 14:2, Mark 6:14).[14] His greatness is also seen in Jesus' identification of John and Elijah (Matt. 17:13). The angel had prophesied to Zechariah that "he will be great before the Lord" (Luke 1:15), and the Gospels bear abundant testimony to the fulfillment of this prophecy.

Thus, we conclude that John was by no means just a "prophet of doom," but a forerunner of the Messiah; a forerunner whose stern insistence upon genuine repentance, although evoking the displeasure and opposition of those who had no need of a physician, brought joy and a foretaste of Messianic blessedness to the multitudes.

It has been established that John's message was one of repentance. This *kerygma* derived its sanction from eschatological considerations. Because the segment of John's ministry that we have recorded is primarily concerned with his encounter with the Pharisees, it is natural to think that he took the same attitude toward his entire following as he took toward that group. But he did not. In Luke 3:10-14 we have preserved a sample of John's preaching on how the command to repent will be worked out in the case of different groups.[15] The multitudes have asked him, "What then shall we do?" To this he answers that those who have more than enough should share with the unfortunate. Taxgatherers are not to exact more than is right. Soldiers are not to "bully or blackmail,"[16] and are to be content with their wages. Thus, the

14 This is especially remarkable because of Herod's Sadducean outlook.

15 This segment is from a different recension of Q or perhaps a completely different source. Matthew confines himself to the sterner aspects.

16 A. M. Hunter, *The Work and Words of Jesus*, p. 35.

manner of life that indicates true repentance is characterized
by thoughtful consideration for others, complete honesty, re-
fusal to use position for personal advantage, and a quiet
contentment with one's lot in life.

It has been suggested that John's positive teaching is something of an anticlimax. It is said to be an *interimsethik* —
"telling men how to make the best of a bad job till the new
day dawns."[17] As this segment of ethical instruction (Luke
3:10-14) is part and parcel of John's *kerygma*, it will be
necessary to investigate this assertion.

That John has no teaching of epoch-making importance is
admitted. However, this is not because he is setting forth an
"ethic of the interval" — suggestions as to how to hang on
until things are set right — but rather because his ministry is
one of preparation and not the propounding of a new and
positive code of ethics. He cries out, "Repent," not, "Learn
my new system of morality."

But should we consider what positive teaching John does
have as being only makeshift and transitory? Are not his
answers the same as would come from an application of Jesus'
Golden Rule or Paul's I Corinthians 13? To be more specific,
is Paul's "contribute to the needs of the saints" (Rom. 12:13)
really any different from John's "share your coats and food"?
Certainly Paul's reprimand to the Corinthians for defraud-
ing each other in law courts (I Cor. 6:7-8) is not basically
different from John's instructions not to extract undue taxes.
And see the parallels to John's advice to the soldiers:

> Do not rob — "Let the thief no longer steal" (Eph. 4:28).
> Do not falsely accuse — "Do not lie to one another" (Col.
> 3:9).
> Be content — "Aspire to live quietly" (I Thess. 4:11).[18]

Thus, there is no qualitative difference between John's "positive teaching" and New Testament ethics in general. (The
power to live accordingly is a separate matter.) If John's ethic

17 T. W. Manson, *The Servant-Messiah*, p. 45.
18 It is interesting that these three admonitions are also parallel to
the last three commandments of the Decalogue: "Ye shall not steal . . .
bear false witness . . . covet." (Exod. 20:15-17).

is an *interimsethik,* we must be prepared to say that so also is the ethic of the entire New Testament.

Finally, those qualities which were found to be peculiar to the concept of heralding, as set forth in the Septuagint, are also characteristic of John's ministry. "He found himself irresistibly caught up by the mighty current of the divine activity in human affairs, appointed to tasks which he dared not refuse, furnished with a message which he must at all costs deliver."[19] His command to repent demanded action. Behind it lay the authority of God. To refuse was to make oneself liable to the most dire consequences. The message was unalterable. Even though it led to his execution, John dared not tamper with it (Matt. 14:1-12, Mark 6:14-28). In every respect John was a true Messianic herald.

19 Manson, *op. cit.,* p. 38.

Chapter Three

THE PREACHING OF JESUS AND THE TWELVE

THE portrayal of Jesus in the Synoptic Gospels is supremely that of one who came "heralding the kingdom of God."[1] This characteristic phase of Jesus' ministry is represented by the verb *kerussein* more than twenty times. Our task is to reconstruct from these sources an accurate account of the nature, content, and characteristics of the preaching of Jesus.

In all but one of the eight separate occasions upon which the verb *kerussein* is used to describe the activity of Jesus, it serves as a resumé of His ministry over a period of time rather than describing what happened in any particular instance.[2] Matthew says that Jesus went about all Galilee "teaching . . . preaching . . . and healing" (4:23). Mark omits "teaching" and alters "healing" to "casting out demons" (1:39).[3] Luke retains only "preaching" (4:44). This suggests that preaching is the most important of the three activities.

Matthew 9:35 repeats the 4:23 summary verbatim except for the initial minor variations and the omission of the final phrase. Matthew 11:1 and Luke 8:1 differ in detail but both portray the over-all ministry of Jesus. Thus "teaching, preach-

1 What this involves is best summarized in Matt. 4:17, Mark 1:14-15. The latter identifies the message as the "gospel of God" — a designation also used with *kerussein* in Matt. 9:35. Elsewhere Jesus is said to preach the "gospel of the kingdom" (Matt. 4:23), or simply "to preach" (Mark 1:38, 39, Luke 4:44, Matt. 11:1, and Luke 8:1). No difference is to be found in the varying expressions.

2 I Pet. 3:19 is the exception.

3 Vincent Taylor's suggestion (*The Gospel According to St. Mark*, p. 184) that ἦλθεν was probably a grammatical correction for an original ἦν, if correct, would provide further support for the view that the verse is a summary. K. L. Schmidt (*Der Rahmen der Geschichte Jesu*, p. 59) labels the verse a "*Sammelbericht*."

28

ing, and healing" was the customary way of summing up the ministry of Jesus.

We are prepared for the prominence of preaching in the ministry of Jesus by His own declaration that it was for this reason that He had come (Mark 1:38). When the ministry of healing threatened to eclipse that of preaching, Jesus drew apart from the clamoring crowd and moved on to the next town. He had come to preach; healing was secondary.

Jesus' concept of His own ministry is further seen in the claim which led to His rejection at Nazareth (Luke 4:16-30). Having entered His home-town synagogue, the "carpenter's son" read the Messianic prophecy of Isaiah 61:1-2, closed the book, and in a moment of silent suspense announced, "Today this scripture has been fulfilled in your hearing" (Luke 4:21). What did He mean?

The prophecy, in its original setting, was the sounding forth of a gracious message to those in captivity. It was the good news of release and restoration. The "acceptable year" was more than just an historical date. It marked the birth of a new era — a time when Yahweh would visit His people and shower them with unprecedented favor and blessing. In the restoration the prophet foresaw the coming Kingdom of God. What he did not see was that "in the providence of God, the stream of that great hope was to run underground for more than five centuries till the decisive time came."[4] The hope was not yet to be realized. It had to wait until the Servant-Messiah would come, whose ministry was the fulfillment of that hope. Thus, Jesus' proclamation was a declaration that at long last this Reign of God had broken in — and that in no abstract sense, but as inseparably involved in His own ministry.

The point to be observed is the prominence of heralding in the ministry of the Servant. He is to proclaim "release to the captives and recovering of sight to the blind" (Luke 4: 18). He is also to proclaim the "acceptable year of the Lord" (v. 19). By equating His ministry with that of the Servant, Jesus is saying that the purpose of His coming is to

---

4 A. M. Hunter, *The Work and Words of Jesus*, p. 72.

make proclamation — to herald the arrival of the Kingdom
of God.

JESUS AND THE KINGDOM OF GOD

The content of Jesus' message must now be examined more
closely. It may be summed up in the phrase "the kingdom of
God." But what, exactly, is the Kingdom of God? And in
what sense was it present in the ministry of Jesus? To arrive
at a satisfactory answer to these questions is to find the key
which unlocks, not only the Gospels, but the entire New
Testament.

Matthew's summary of Jesus' Galilean ministry ("Repent,
for the kingdom of heaven is at hand," 4:17) is an abbrevia-
tion of that given by Mark ("The time is fulfilled, and the
kingdom of God is at hand; repent, and believe in the gospel,"
1:15). Matthew omits the first clause because he has just dealt
with fulfillment (v. 14); the final clause, because it is implied in what precedes.[5] We are left with two essential items:
an ethical demand, and its eschatological sanction. Which
element takes logical precedence depends upon whether one
views the total announcement from an indicative or an imperative standpoint.

What repentance means, raises no problem. It is not so
much an intellectual "change of mind," as the Greek suggests, as it is a complete reorientation of the moral disposition. It takes its coloring from the Old Testament *shub*, "to
turn." However, to understand what the Kingdom of God
means is decidedly more difficult. That it could be announced without explanation shows that the concept was fa-
miliar (even though the exact phraseology is not to be
found). Yet the fact that the nature of the Kingdom had later
to be illustrated by numerous parables indicates that the
current understanding needed modification.

If we look to the history of interpretation for the answer,
we may come away more bewildered than helped. Prior to

5 This tendency of Matthew to retain only the essential elements of
Mark's redundant style is illustrated by W. C. Allen, *Matthew* (*International Critical Commentary*), pp. xxiv-xxv.

the allegorizing of Origen, the Kingdom of God seems to have been understood in an eschatological frame of reference. It was not the Church, but something prepared for the Church.[6] However, Origen promptly "de-eschatologized" the concept,[7] and Augustine equated it with the *Ecclesia Catholica*, which interpretation pervaded medieval thought. The Reformers merely shifted the identification to the "community of the elect" and loosely understood the Kingdom as the reign of God in the hearts of the redeemed.

Thus the way was prepared for the influential German theologian Albert Ritschl (1822-89) to define the Kingdom as "the organization of humanity through action inspired by love."[8] Ritschl's non-eschatological interpretation dominated theological thought in the last half of the nineteenth century,[9] and still lingers with some of the more recent writers who are reluctant to give up the pleasant thought of the Kingdom as an "inner spiritual reality."[10]

We are indebted to the Ritschlian school for having revived interest in what always should have been a crucial concept. However, their interpretation of the Kingdom cannot be accepted for several important reasons. For instance, where in the Old Testament does one find the background for such a view? It is foreign to Hebraic thought. Or, why did the first four centuries of Christianity nowhere equate the Kingdom and the Church? It may also be added that Ritschl's interpretation overlooked the uniform evidence of the Scripture that the Kingdom is supernatural — it is God's activity.

The pendulum of thought took a violent swing in the "consistent eschatology" of Weiss (son-in-law of Ritschl) and Schweitzer. The Kingdom was no longer thought of as a gentle influence being presently realized in man's heart, but as wholly future — the catastrophic breaking in of the future

6 The *Didache*, 10. 5.

7 *De Principiis*, ii. 11. 2-3.

8 Ritschl, *The Christian Doctrine of Justification and Reconciliation*, p. 12.

9 Ritschl's influence is seen in such writers as Harnack (*What Is Christianity?*) and A. B. Bruce (*The Kingdom of God*).

10 Cf. *The Historic Mission of Jesus*, pp. 115ff., by C. J. Cadoux.

order. This ingenious construction was destined to force upon all subsequent scholars the necessity of treating seriously the eschatological element in the teaching of Jesus. It proved, however, to be more of a corrective measure than a final solution. While all must start with Schweitzer, he treads the greater part of his journey alone.[11]

These two radically opposed interpretations have brought into focus the paradoxical nature of the Scriptural data. The Kingdom of God is both present and future. The problem is one of integration. How are the eschatological elements in the sayings of Jesus related to the non-eschatological? It is no answer simply to treat the apocalyptic as a "bold imaginative way" of asserting the certain triumph of a present reality. Nor can all the eschatological sayings be attributed to the creative genius of the primitive Church. What is needed is a genuine synthesis.

Otto's work, *The Kingdom of God and the Son of Man* (1934), represents the first major movement away from Schweitzer. Although the Kingdom is mostly future, it is also proleptically present in the sense of anticipation. Gloege comes closer to balancing the two elements.[12] The Kingdom is present because God's rule is not only eternal, but also because in Jesus it is breaking into the present. It is future in that it is not yet fully manifested on earth as in heaven. Perhaps the best known approach is that of C. H. Dodd and "realized eschatology." Here the *eschaton* (the final purpose which gives meaning to history) has moved from "the sphere of expectation into that of realized experience."[13]

This wide range of interpretation on what is acknowledged to be a pivotal concept necessitates a reinvestigation of the Biblical material. To do full justice to such an undertaking would lead us far astray from the aim of this chapter. All that will be attempted is to suggest the proper lines of development.

11 Even Weiss, in his later works, admitted the non-eschatological nature of certain sayings. Cf. R. Newton Flew, "Jesus and the Kingdom of God," *Expository Times*, XLVI (Feb. 1935), p. 215.

12 G. Gloege, *Das Reich Gottes und Kirche im Neuen Testament.*

13 C. H. Dodd, *The Parables of the Kingdom*, p. 50.

Translation has its peculiar difficulties, and one of them is that exact linguistic equivalents are virtually non-existent. The English word "kingdom" and the Greek βασιλεία, as translating the Aramaic *malkutha* (the word undoubtedly spoken by Jesus), illustrate this. Both have distinct associations that are foreign to the original concept. As a result, interpreters have wrongly described the Kingdom of God in terms of a realm, or subjects in that realm, instead of retaining the primary meaning of "kingly rule" or "sovereignty." At present, however, there is almost unanimous agreement among the scholars that "realm" and "people" are secondary aspects, and "kingly rule" is regulative.[14]

Several factors have led to this conclusion. The most important has been the simple observation of the meaning of the word in its original milieu. In Jewish literature, *malkuth* always means "kingly rule."[15] This is admirably illustrated by the Targum of Onkelos where Exodus 15:18, "The Lord shall reign for ever and ever," is paraphrased by, "His *malkuth* stands for ever and ever." In Rabbinic literature, the Kingdom of God is God's kingship. The frequent phrase "to take the yoke of the Kingdom of God on oneself" meant to accept the Torah as God's revealed will, to recite daily the *Shema* (Deut. 6:4), and to acknowledge God as Lord and King.[16]

In the New Testament this same abstract quality can be found. The nobleman of Luke 19:11-27 went into a far country to receive "kingly power" (RSV), which he exercised over his subjects upon returning. Revelation 17:12 speaks of ten kings who have not yet received "royal power" (RSV), but are to receive "authority as kings." Taylor concludes that in the overwhelming majority of Jesus' sayings about the Kingdom (in more than fifty of the sixty references), "the thought is that of the Reign or Rule of God."[17] When we also remem-

---

14 K. L. Schmidt, in *Theologisches Wörterbuch zum Neuen Testament*, I, 582; G. Gloege, *op. cit.*, pp. 49-58; R. N. Flew, *The Idea of Perfection in Christian Theology*, pp. 8-40; Otto, *op. cit.*, pp. 53f.

15 G. Dalman, *The Words of Jesus*, p. 94.

16 Cf. Strack-Billerbeck, *Kommentar zum Neuen Testament*, I, 173ff, for examples.

17 V. Taylor, *Jesus and His Sacrifice*, p. 9.

ber that nowhere in the first four centuries of Christianity are the Church and "the kingdom" equated, we must concede that modern philologists are more than warranted in their insistence that God's Kingdom in its primary sense is His "kingly rule" or "sovereign action."

In addition to the linguistic evidence, we have the history of the concept as it runs through Hebrew thought. Although the exact term, Kingdom of God, is not to be found in the Old Testament, the "root idea, that God is king" and that "His kingly rule will be manifested to the confusion of all evil, is the burden of all prophecy."[18]

In one sense, God's sovereignty is absolute and eternal. He always has and always will be King whether man is rebellious or submissive. This basic principle is an integral part of the Hebrew view of God. "The Lord will reign for ever and ever" (Exod. 15:18) sang Moses and the people. "Thy dominion endures throughout all generations" (Ps. 145:13b) echoes the Psalmist.[19]

In another sense God's timeless sovereignty was viewed as being realized in the religious life of Israel in so far as they acknowledged it and accepted its obligations. This view of God's *malkuth* was acceptable while Israel was flourishing, but how could it be vindicated when Israel fell under alien rule and the Davidic monarchy had seemingly disappeared? Was God still ruling in history? Although almost overpowered by the darkness of the exile, the flickering flame of Israel's hope was destined to persevere. Fanned by prophetic testimony and fed by apocalyptic speculation, the confidence in God's "kingly rule" began to burn with a new brilliance. But now the emphasis was shifted to the future aspect. Before long a new era would dawn when man would no longer be at variance with the rule of God. Although God's sovereignty was for the moment veiled, there would soon be a day of open manifestation — a day when God would decisively intervene

18 C. H. Dodd, "Jesus as Teacher and Prophet," *Mysterium Christi*, p. 62.

19 Extra-canonical Jewish literature tells the same story. Cf. T. W. Manson, *The Teaching of Jesus*, p. 136.

in the affairs of man and establish His rule in the sight of all.[20]

It should be noted that these three phases are in no sense mutually exclusive. Their interrelation has been succinctly stated by A. M. Hunter, who writes, "The eternal sovereignty of God, now acknowledged in Israel, will one day be effectively manifested in the world."[21] Yet, as a background for Jesus' thought, it is the eschatological idea that predominates. When He proclaimed, "The kingdom of God is at hand," He was speaking eschatologically. His *kerygma* was the climactic culmination of the Jewish expectation. Yet this expectation (at least, in its prevailing form) needed modification. It would, therefore, be most premature for us to answer the original question, "What is the Kingdom of God?" before investigating what new light the teaching of Jesus throws on the subject. It is what *Jesus* meant, not what His contemporaries understood, that is of crucial significance. This is bound up with the further question, "In what sense did the Kingdom *come* with Jesus?" When these two aspects are properly related we shall better understand the real thrust of Jesus' proclamation.

Much ink has been spilled over the meaning of ἐγγίζειν in Jesus' announcement, "The kingdom of God *has come/drawn near*" (Mark 1:15). Dodd argues that Mark's summary is to be taken in the same sense as the Q saying, "The kingdom of God has come upon you (ἔφθασεν)" (Matt. 12:28, Luke 11:30).[22] This "expresses in the most vivid and forcible way the fact that the Kingdom of God has actually arrived."[23] Further, in the LXX, ἐγγίζειν is sometimes used to translate the Hebrew *naga'* and the Aramaic *m'ta*, both of which mean "to arrive."

Against Dodd, Campbell argues that the LXX gives no good

---

20 Dodd (*The Parables of the Kingdom*, p. 39n.) writes, "The eschatological idea of the Kingdom of God seems to arise naturally from primitive Hebrew conceptions, under the influence of prophetic teaching and of outward events."

21 Hunter, *The Work and Words of Jesus*, p. 70.

22 Dodd, *Parables*, pp. 43-45.

23 *Ibid.*, p. 43n. Cf. also his chapter in *Mysterium Christi*, p. 66, n.1.

evidence that the perfect, ἤγγικεν, ever means "has come,"
and that ἔφθασεν may well mean "has drawn near."[24] Subsequent treatments of the problem[25] show that, although Professor Dodd may or may not be completely right, at least the
matter will have to be dealt with on grounds other than bare
philology. The problem is theological as well as linguistic.

What then are the reasons for asserting that the Kingdom
of God has come?

First, there are a number of reasonably direct statements
to the effect that the Kingdom is a present reality. When
accused of casting out demons by Beelzebub, Jesus corrects
the logic of His critics and adds, "But if it is by the finger
of God that I cast out demons, then the kingdom of God has
come upon you" (Luke 11:20). The argument is clear and
forceful: (1) I cast out demons; (2) since it cannot be by
Satan's power, it must be by God's; (3) therefore, God's Kingdom, viz., His sovereignty in action, is here. Again, in Luke
16:16 and Matthew 11:12, whether we understand the Kingdom as "suffering violence" or as "exercising force,"[26] it still
remains that since John the Baptist the Kingdom is a present
reality.[27]

In addition, there are present-tense statements about the
Kingdom which imply its presence. For example, "Blessed are
you poor, for yours is the kingdom of God" (Luke 6:20), and

24 J. Y. Campbell, "The Kingdom of God Has Come," *Expository Times*,
XLVIII (Nov. 1936), pp. 91-94. He also argues that the use of ἤγγικεν
in the proclamation of John the Baptist (Matt. 3:2), even if Matthaean
in origin, disproves Dodd's point.

This is a telling observation.

25 C. H. Dodd, *Expository Times*, XLVIII (Dec. 1936), pp. 138-42;
J. M. Creed, *Expository Times*, XLVIII (Jan. 1937), pp. 184-85; K. W.
Clark, *Journal of Biblical Literature*, Sept. 1940, pp. 17-26; M. Black,
Expository Times, LXIII (June 1952), pp. 289-90; W. R. Hutton, *Ex-
pository Times*, LXIV (Dec. 1952), pp. 89-91.

26 Taking βιάζεται as passive voice in the first instance, or as middle
voice in the second.

27 Jesus' statement, "Behold, the kingdom of God is in the midst of
you" (Luke 17:21), although frequently used to prove a present Kingdom, may rather mean that the future Kingdom will come to pass sud-
denly and without signs. Cf. T. W. Manson, *The Sayings of Jesus*, p. 304.

Jesus' remark to the wise scribe, "You are not far from the kingdom of God" (Mark 12:34).

Secondly, a great number of the sayings of Jesus presuppose a new era — the age of fulfillment that prophets and kings had eagerly anticipated (Luke 10:23-24, Matt. 13:16-17). Something (the noun is neuter, thus not "someone") greater than either Solomon or Jonah has come (Luke 11:31-32). Satan has been bound (Mark 2:19). It is an occasion for feasting and gladness (Mark 2:19). To John the Baptist's doubting question rings back the answer, "The blind receive their sight . . . the deaf hear . . . the poor have good news preached to them" (Luke 7:22). Jesus is everywhere conscious that His ministry is ushering in a new age. He thrusts decision on all men (Luke 11:23, Matt. 12:30) even though some may take offense (Luke 7:23). In fact, it is only against this background of an inbreaking Kingdom that the over-all tenor of Jesus' sayings can be understood at all.

Finally, both the parables and the miracles testify to the reality of God's present reign. The Parables of Growth are particularly relevant at this point. Here the primary emphasis does not lie upon the contrast between small beginnings and large results, much less upon the length of time involved, but rather, "upon the fact that forces have been set in motion which inevitably move to fruition."[28] Dodd has used this group of parables as major evidence in his case for "realized eschatology."[29] The Parable of the Self-growing Seed (Mark 4:26-29) clearly shows the Kingdom of God as a present reality that will, in God's time and by His power, be finally brought to complete fruition.

The miracles, also, witness to the here-and-now character of God's reign. The days are past when it was possible to regard

28 John Bright, *The Kingdom of God*, p. 219, n. 3.

29 Dodd, *Parables*, pp. 175-94. However, note that he represents the arrival of the *eschaton* as the harvest of a long previous growth, rather than the divine sowing of a new power. Jeremias' phrase, *sich realisierende Eschatologie* ("an eschatology that is in process of realization") is a more accurate designation (*The Parables of Jesus*, p. 159). Jeremias notes that Dodd has agreed with him in principle at this point (*op. cit.*, p. 159, n. 2).

them as a group of Hellenistic wonder stories or as first-century anticipations of modern psychotherapy. They are now recognized as an integral part of the Messiah's mission. They are "the Kingdom of God in action."[30] They mean that the powers of evil, which have invaded every level of life, are going down in defeat.

Yet, while the Kingdom is present, there is ample proof that it is also future. A few examples will suffice.

Jesus taught His disciples to pray for the coming of the Kingdom on earth as it is in heaven (Matt. 6:10). This is certainly a prayer for a future realization. In connection with this verse T. W. Manson observes, "In the fullest sense the Kingdom is still future and an object of hope rather than experience."[31] Jesus' declaration at the Last Supper, "I shall not drink again of the fruit of the vine until that day when I drink it new in the kingdom of God" (Mark 14:25), is strong evidence of a future Kingdom.[32] When Jesus was about to enter Jerusalem for the last time, He had to tell a parable of a nobleman who was going into a *far* country to receive kingly authority, in order to disabuse their minds of the false notion that "the kingdom of God was to appear immediately" (Luke 19:11). Matthew 25 speaks of a Kingdom that will be inherited after the return of the Son of Man in judgment (Matt. 25:31-34).

There is no need to multiply the evidence. It is quite clear that while the Kingdom is a present possession, it is also, in a very real sense, a future inheritance. "All attempts . . . to explain these two meanings of Kingdom of God by eliminating one of them have failed."[33]

How then shall we resolve the dilemma? When we reflect for a moment that God's Kingdom, in the broadest sense, is an eternal reign, we realize that its "coming" in the ministry of

30 Hunter, *op. cit.*, p. 74. Cf. also Schmidt, in *Theologisches Wörterbuch zum Neuen Testament*, I, 584-585), where the driving out of demons is seen as the inbreaking of the Kingdom of God.

31 Manson, *Sayings*, p. 169.

32 V. Taylor (*The Life and Ministry of Jesus*, p. 68) cites this verse as the strongest proof of a future Kingdom.

33 Jackson and Lake, *The Beginnings of Christianity*, I, 280.

Jesus is not something totally unrelated to the past.[34] Nor did it come so completely that any future aspect is automatically ruled out. It should be understood in terms of a crucial and unique manifestation of God's dynamic reign. The Kingdom of God is God acting. God is to be conceived of as Active Will. His reign is likened to someone *doing* something. As a clue to the nature of this activity, R. N. Flew draws attention to the phrase, "the finger of God."[35] This phrase is used in the Old Testament only in reference to certain epochal events that for the Hebrew mind illumined the meaning of history. The creation of the heavens was the work of God's fingers (Ps. 8:3). It was by the "finger of God" that the Israelites were taken from Egyptian bondage (Exod. 8:19). The Law was written by the "finger of God" (Exod. 31:18). It was not by accident that Jesus adopted this phrase, thus defining His ministry as another act of the "finger of God" (Luke 11:20). But, whereas past events had been but preliminary skirmishes, this was the crucial battle. The casting out of demons was proof that the "strong man" had been mortally wounded. This was the decisive hour in the spiritual history of the world. The uniqueness of the Kingdom lay not only in that it had become a present reality, but also in that it was redemptive action. In and through Jesus Christ, God's timeless sovereignty was invading history and victoriously waging redemptive warfare against the evil powers. The Kingdom of God had come.

Not only does the New Testament equate the Kingdom of God with the Kingdom of Christ, but also with Christ Him-

34 The question of exactly when the Kingdom came in reference to the ministry of Jesus is not vital to our present study. Dodd's view, that the decisive event had already occurred in the lifetime of Jesus, is strongly attacked by R. H. Fuller, who maintains that such an interpretation destroys the cruciality of the Cross (*The Mission and Achievement of Jesus*, pp. 48-49). Manson (*Teaching*, p. 130) equates the coming of the Kingdom with Peter's confession. It seems to me unlikely that Jesus' life-death-resurrection will lend itself to such penetrating chronological exactness. Certainly, to identify the coming of the Kingdom with the Christ-event as a whole does not blur any of the essential features.

35 Flew, *Jesus and His Church*, pp. 32-33.

self.[36] Jesus is the Kingdom.[37] How then is the Kingdom yet future? In the sense that the universal vindication of God's redemptive act in Christ Jesus awaits the final shudder of the enemy now mortally wounded. Or, to change the figure, the dynamic forces set in motion at the Kingdom's decisive coming will reach their complete fruition only in the future.

We may sum up by saying that while Jesus took up the Jewish expectation of a coming Kingdom, it was not first without "depoliticizing" it. Jesus taught that the Kingdom of God was a present reality — not in the sense of the immediate destruction of all evil, but as a wedge driven into the world, the resulting tensions of which would inevitably effect a complete cleavage.

Perhaps now we can venture an answer to our original question as to what the Kingdom of God meant for Jesus. In the broadest sense, it is God's eternal sovereignty, dynamically conceived, which invaded the realm of evil powers and won the decisive victory in and through Jesus Christ, which victory will be eventually complete and fully acknowledged by all mankind. This was the essential content of Jesus' kerygma — the good news that He heralded in that momentous hour.

PREACHING AND TEACHING

Considerable attention has been given to the content of Jesus' proclamation. And this is right, for preaching was of primary significance in the ministry of Jesus. However, the summary statements (Matt. 4:23, 9:35) list "teaching" and "healing" as well. Since these two activities are integrally related to and involved in the total proclamation, they must be studied for the insight they give into the essential nature of the preaching of Jesus.

Professor Dodd has drawn a rather definite line of demarcation between the kerygma, which he calls "the public proclamation of Christianity to the non-Christian world," and

---

36 Cf. Schmidt, in Theologisches Wörterbuch zum Neuen Testament, I, 581, 590-91.

37 Modern research has acknowledged Origen's word αὐτοβασιλεία and Marcion's phrase, "In the Gospel the Kingdom of God is Christ himself" (Schmidt, op. cit., I, 591) as the ultimate solution.

the *didache*, "ethical instruction."[38] Those responding to the *kerygma* are said to have then been instructed in the *didache*. In a later work, Dodd distinguishes the *didache* more exactly as "a traditional body of ethical teaching given to converts from paganism to Christianity."[39] What we would here question is the assertion that in the Gospels there is preserved a "clear distinction between preaching and teaching."[40]

In fairness it should be mentioned that Dodd everywhere assumes the dependence of the *didache* upon the *kerygma*. His desire for analytical clarity, however, has resulted in too great a cleavage between the two. We shall attempt to show that they are continuous and to some degree overlapping.

Any clear-cut distinction is blurred by the fact that "heralding" is not such a closely defined concept as to allow no synonyms. In Mark 1:38 Jesus says that He came "in order to preach," while the parallel in Luke says He was sent "to bring the good news." Again, in the report of the sending out of the Twelve, Mark says that in addition to healings and exorcisms, "they preached" (Mark 6:12), while Luke uses "preached the good news" (Luke 9:6).[41] If the *kerygma* shows a certain flexibility at this point, it may well resist too strict a comparison with other concepts.

More telling, however, is the direct evidence. Matthew 4:23 says that Jesus was "teaching in the synagogues"; the other writers give His activity as "preaching" (Mark 1:39, Luke 4:44). Although we cannot equate the two, since Matthew goes on to list "preaching," we can at least say that "preaching," as used by Mark and Luke, is sufficiently broad to include "teaching." It should be added that since the activity generally associated with the synagogue was "teaching," the synagogue "preaching" recorded by Mark and Luke seems rather out of place unless the two have a good deal in common.

Again, Jesus' Capernaum ministry is described by Mark as teaching (1:21, 22, 27), exorcism (1:23-28, 34), and healing

38 Dodd, *The Apostolic Preaching*, p. 7.
39 Dodd, *Gospel and Law*, p. 15.
40 Dodd, *The Apostolic Preaching*, p. 7.
41 In both instances Mark uses κηρύσσειν while Luke writes εὐαγγελίσασθαι.

(1:29-31, 32-34). Yet 1:38 indicates that Jesus viewed His
ministry there as one of preaching. Consider also that the
famous proclamation, "Repent, for the kingdom of God is at
hand" (Matt. 4:17, Mark 1:14-15), becomes, in the Third Gospel, "and he *taught* in their synagogues" (Luke 4:15). From
this ambiguity of expression we may judge that Professor Dodd
has overstated his case in reference to any "clear distinction
between preaching and teaching" in the Gospels.[42]

If the Synoptic evidence does not lend itself to such clear-
cut categories, what, then, is the relation between preaching
and teaching, and in what sense do they overlap?

The Nazareth incident (Luke 4:16-30) will illustrate the
point well. When Jesus finished reading the Servant prophecy,
He proclaimed, "Today this scripture has been fulfilled in your
hearing." This is "proclamation" in its unique sense. But
was that all He said? Hardly. They "bore witness" (v. 22)
that the reports about His greatness as a teacher were true.
They wondered at His "gracious words" (v. 22). All this sup-
poses a detailed explanation of what was involved in the basic
proclamation. They needed to be *taught* the implications of
the announcement — especially since it was the local carpenter's
son who was making the claim. Thus, teaching is the expound-
ing in detail of that which is proclaimed.[43] The relation is
that of an axiom to its explanation and application. As such,
the connection is logical rather than chronological. Or, to
change the figure, *kerygma* is foundation and *didache* is super-

42 G. C. Stead, reviewing Dodd's *Gospel and Law* (*Journal of Theological Studies,* IV [1953], 139-41), concludes that Dodd's neat distinction
between *kerygma* and *didache* is a "rather drastic simplification" (p.
141). John J. Vincent ("Didactic Kerygma in the Synoptic Gospels,"
Scottish Journal of Theology, X [Sept. '57], 262-73) arguing along the
same line, goes so far as to say, "The only κήρυγμα, of which we are
entitled to speak on the basis of the Synoptics is 'a didactic kerygma'"
(p. 271). Cf. also H. G. Wood's contribution in *New Testament Essays*
(studies in memory of T. W. Manson).

43 Flew (*Jesus and His Church,* p. 112) notes that this incident comes
between two references to Jesus' teaching in synagogues (Luke 4:15 and
31 with v. 38), and concludes that Luke would certainly not have excluded such preaching from the content of His synagogue teaching elsewhere.

structure; but no building is complete without both. It is only when they are ideally conceived that teaching and preaching can be taken as entirely distinct. In actual practice they overlap, and may be so intermingled that one can hardly ever say, "Now this is preaching," or, "This, on the other hand, is teaching."[44] All *didache* is based on *kerygma,* and it may be seriously doubted whether any *kerygma* ever stands without some measure of explanatory *didache*.

It is not denied that there may well have emerged in the early Church a distinctive missionary proclamation as over against a body of ethical instruction. All that is here maintained is that "teaching" and "preaching," as used in the Synoptics, do not admit of such a sharp distinction. Instead, we find a natural overlapping of both concept and terminology.

PREACHING AND HEALING

Turning now to the third characteristic phase of Jesus' ministry, what can we say of healing in relation to preaching? To answer this question, we must first determine the nature and function of miracle as found in its Gospel setting.

The New Testament everywhere assumes both the possibility and occurrence of miracles. Jesus implied that "mighty works" were an admitted part of His activity (Luke 10:13), and that God's supernatural power knew no limits (Mark 9:23). The importance of miracle in the mind of the Evangelists is seen in that approximately one third of Mark deals directly or indirectly with it. Even more striking is the fact that if the Passion narrative is omitted, then about forty-seven percent of Mark deals with miracle. It is no incidental strand in the total fabric.

There are three principal New Testament words for miracles. Δυνάμεις, the plural of the word meaning "physical power,"

44 This relation between historical fact and ethical implication is so close that one strand of the latter has actually found its way into Dodd's *kerygma,* for what is repentance but the ethical demand for moral reorientation (most certainly *didache*) based upon the historical events of Christ's life, death, and resurrection (cf. *The Apostolic Preaching,* p. 23)? Even at the core, his elsewhere sharp distinction is not maintained.

stresses the Biblical concept that miracles are the manifestation of the power of God, operating dynamically within the
historical process. It emphasizes the source and nature of
the miraculous. τέρας is a less frequent designation (three
times in the Gospel) and emphasizes the extraordinary character of the miracle. It is significant that this designation is
never used in the New Testament apart from the third word,
σημεῖον — a miracle regarded as "an outward (visible) indication of secret power or truth."[45] This latter word is by
far the most frequent (forty-eight times in the Gospels, seventeen of which are in John) and suggests the function of miracle.

A simple, but workable, definition of a miracle in the Biblical sense is, "an event which happens in a manner contrary to
the regularly observed processes of nature."[46] There was a
time when science conceived of nature as operating in accordance with a system of inviolable laws. The dogma of the fixity
of nature made miracles unthinkable. During this era, any
explanation of the miraculous, no matter how ludicrous, was
markedly more palatable than the medieval view of supernatural intervention.

This view, however, was destined to be radically revised.
Science began to overcome one "impossibility" after the other.
In 1930 Sir James Jeans wrote that the universe was "more
like a great thought than like a great machine."[47]

Religious thought, however, was more embarrassed by the
"explaining away" of Rationalism than by the changing trend
of science. Thus the 1900s ushered in the age of New Enlight-
enment. Miracles did not occur; yet, you must not explain
them away. What then? They are supernatural — that is, they
are natural events religiously regarded. It soon became obvious that Modernism could not completely evade its own
charge of "explaining away." Meanwhile, science discarded its
last inclination to hold to a closed system, and religious thought
is now realizing that had it acted as a co-worker instead of a

45 Souter, *A Pocket Lexicon to the Greek New Testament*, p. 234.
46 A. Richardson, "Miracle," in *A Theological Word Book of the Bible*,
p. 152.
47 *The Mysterious Universe*, p. 148.

pupil it would have been a hundred years ahead in the study of miracles.

Before we set forth a positive approach, a word should be said about the view of Form Criticism that the miracle-stories were told to prove Jesus' superiority as a wonder-worker. Bultmann, after collecting a number of non-Christian parallels to the Gospel miracles, concludes that the latter "arise in the same atmosphere as the Jewish and Hellenistic miracle-stories."[48] "Faith," for the one healed, is merely trust in the wonder-worker. The Evangelists used the stories as proofs of Jesus' supernatural power, which power functioned more or less automatically. Dibelius, in essential agreement, stresses the "secular" nature of the "tales."[49] In the hands of a special group of "story-tellers," they are used in the propagation of the new cult.

Against this view (which, incidentally, perpetuates the traditional error that the miracles were included in the tradition for their "evidential value") can be marshaled a number of weighty objections. For example: Has not an exaggerated significance been given to the discovery of the "form" of miracle-stories? Would not the account of any healing — be it ancient or modern — include (1) the circumstances, (2) the actual healing, and (3) the impression on the onlookers? But this is not proof that it "arises in the same atmosphere" as the accounts of other healings. Hellenistic parallels are not to be denied, but against Bultmann, who claims they help us to understand the appearance of miracle-stories in the Gospel tradition,[50] Taylor rightly argues that in effect they display the distinctiveness of those associated with Jesus.[51] "Where," asks Taylor, "does He [Jesus] bring a piece from the gravestone of a virgin to a diseased foot?"[52] In drawing attention to the "technique," Form Criticism overlooks the fact that in the Bible characteristic actions have a particular significance. It

---

48 R. Bultmann, *Die Geschichte der synoptischen Tradition* (2d ed.), p. 246.

49 Dibelius, *From Tradition to Gospel*, pp. 70ff.

50 Bultmann, *op. cit.*, p. 253.

51 Vincent Taylor, *The Formation of the Gospel Tradition*, pp. 128-31.

52 *Ibid.*, p. 129.

would be most strange if they had been omitted. Furthermore, what shall we say of those Biblical miracle-stories where no action is recorded?

Is it not unfair to the total portrait of Jesus to isolate the miracle-stories and in them to see Him as nothing more than a wonder-worker? In fact, can this be reconciled at all with the fact that on more than one occasion He flatly refused to perform as a doer of the miraculous?[53]   Had He only been a wonder-worker, He would certainly have silenced the exorcist who was casting out demons in His name (Mark 9:38-40). Professional jealousy is a powerful motive.

That form critics experience considerable difficulty in maintaining a distinction between the purpose of paradigms and that of miracle-stories suggests that alien categories are being forced upon the material.   It is also obvious that content plays more of a role in the process of division than Form Criticism cares to admit.   Certain unanimously recognized paradigms bear a far greater formal affinity to miracle-stories than to other paradigms.   In the account of the Syrophoenician's daughter (Mark 7:24-31) the attempt to divide by form breaks down completely.

We must conclude, therefore, that the presuppositions of Form Criticism in regard to miracles have led to faulty conclusions.

The modern approach to miracles has been ably set forth by Alan Richardson in his book *The Miracle-Stories of the Gospels*. All that is necessary here is to emphasize those points that are particularly relevant to our problem of relating healing and preaching.

Richardson begins by reviewing the theological convictions concerning the nature of God that were held by those who framed the miracle-stories of the Gospel tradition. For them God was living, personal, and active within history. He was the original and only source of power. Hence, for them "miracles" presented no problem.   In the New Testament, power

53 In the Temptation, Jesus refused to indulge in crowd-gathering stunts (Matt. 4:5-7).   He refused to give the Pharisees proof of His Messiahship (Mark 8:11-13).   Even on the cross He refused to come down and gain a following (Matt. 27:42).

is constantly ascribed to God. This power, however, is veiled for the present. It is revealed only to faith. It is experienced in and through Christ, who is the power of God in action. Against this background, miracles are to be seen as "a revelation of the power and of the saving purpose of God."[54]

This re-emphasis on the theological understanding of the compilers makes it clear that the much-discussed question, "Did they actually happen?" should no longer receive such priority. Rather, we must ask, "Why were they so prominent in the setting forth of the Gospel story?" When this primary question is answered, says Richardson, the secondary question will have answered itself.[55]

The Synoptics bear unanimous testimony that both Jesus and the early Church viewed miracles as evidence of the in-breaking Kingdom of God.[56] They testified to the dawn of a New Age. Against this background of the fulfillment of Old Testament prophecy, Mark places his entire series of miraculous happenings.

From this it follows that the working of miracles was nothing else but an integral part of the Kingdom proclamation — an essential part of the *kerygma* itself. Not only was the Kingdom formally proclaimed, but this announcement was also explained, and — witness the miracles — acted out. Seen in this way, preaching, teaching, and healing are not three separate activities of Jesus' ministry, but rather three inseparable elements in the making known to man that the long-awaited time had come and God was acting decisively in Christ Jesus for the redemption of mankind.

It must be added that while miracles were in one sense Messianic signs, they were not intended to compel belief. They were not signs to an unbelieving people (Mark 8:12), but only for those who had eyes to see. Those with the insight

54 Richardson, *The Miracle-Stories of the Gospels,* p. 17.
55 *Ibid.,* p. 36.
56 Cf. especially the Beelzebub Controversy in both Mark (3:22-30) and Q (Matt. 12:24-32, Luke 11:17-20). Matthew's change of "the finger of God" to "the Spirit of God" emphasizes the conviction that the working of miracles was by the power of the Holy Spirit. Cf. also Luke 4:18ff.

of faith[57] would see the miracles as prophetic signs — "symbolical acts which convey in a dramatized form essential Christological teaching."[58]

From a slightly different standpoint, miracles are seen as external indications of the supreme Messianic miracle, viz., the deliverance of man from the evil powers. At the same time, it is equally correct to say that they are the Kingdom itself — that is, the "Kingdom of God in action."

We conclude that since miracles are "not seals attached to the document, but parts of the document itself,"[59] they bear an organic and inseparable relationship to the Messianic *kerygma*. The revelation of God acting redemptively in history is one; its methods of self-communication are various.

JESUS' USE OF KERUSSEIN

Let us now consider how the verb *kerussein* was used by Jesus Himself. It is first found in the M account of the sending out of the Twelve. Jesus sends them to the lost sheep of the house of Israel with the instructions, "Preach as you go, saying, 'The kingdom of heaven is at hand'" (Matt. 10:7). This oral proclamation is to be accompanied by healings and exorcisms.

The nature of this preaching mission is strikingly similar to the classical concept of heralding. The Twelve are divinely commissioned by the Son of Man. Their message is to be the same as His (Matt. 4:17, Mark 1:15). His power is delegated to them, even to the extent of raising the dead (Matt. 10:8).[60] The urgency of the mission is reflected in the charge not to be encumbered with extra equipment nor to waste time on those who do not respond. The proclamation has an official ring.

---

57 Note Cairns' strong emphasis on faith as the condition of the signs (*The Faith That Rebels*, pp. 71-85).

58 Richardson, *op. cit.*, p. 57.

59 Cairns, *op. cit.*, p. 70.

60 Although absent from Matthew and Luke, this phrase is strongly attested (B C D, all Latin MSS, Syriac, Coptic, and Ethiopic). It is omitted only in late MSS (L, Sahidic, and Armenian), undoubtedly because copyists realized that no instance of raising the dead had been recorded.

It is to be delivered courteously, but firmly. If it is refused, the disciples are to withdraw, shaking the dust from their feet as an indication of severance of fellowship. On this mission the Twelve are acting as official heralds of God. Their commission is to "proclaim" the arrival of God's sovereign Reign.

A second use of *kerussein* by Jesus has to do with His pronouncement concerning hypocrisy: "Whatever you have said in the dark shall be heard in the light, and what you have whispered in private rooms shall be proclaimed upon the housetops" (Luke 12:3). Here again we are met with the essential characteristic of heralding, viz., oral proclamation. The verb *kerussein* is not at all out of place in representing the shouting from housetops.

Matthew (10:27) has restated the saying and uses it in the commissioning of the Twelve. Here it becomes the instruction to proclaim in public what they have been told in private. Although the mission of the Twelve included an element of teaching (Matt. 11:1), it was basically an extension of the *kerygma* that the Kingdom of God was at hand.

In Matthew 24:14 Jesus says that "this gospel of the kingdom" must be universally heralded before the end comes. As a chief condition for the final consummation, it becomes charged with a sense of urgency. The early Church was given to believe that a faithful and urgent heralding of the Gospel would in a sense hasten the end.[61]

Jesus also speaks of the Gospel being heralded in the whole world in connection with the woman with the alabaster box of ointment (Matt. 26:13, Mark 14:9).

Finally, in the Lucan post-resurrection narrative, Jesus causes His disciples to understand that the Old Testament foretold not only the death and resurrection of God's Annointed, but also (by way of encouragement) that "repentance unto the forgiveness of sins"[62] was to be proclaimed to all nations (Luke 24:47). Here again we see the close relationship be-

---

61 Cf. II Pet. 3:12.

62 Following the Koine and Caesarean texts, the RSV translates "repentance *and* forgiveness." This, of course, does not affect the point in question.

tween heralding and repentance. It will be remembered that
John the Baptist preached, Repent! (Matt. 3:2). So also did
Jesus (Matt. 4:17). Mark says concerning the preaching mission of the Twelve that "they went out and preached that
men should repent" (Mark 6:12). And now the risen Lord
adds that "repentance" is to be proclaimed to all nations. Thus
repentance is a crucial element in the Gospel proclamation and
the true goal of all valid preaching.

The remaining uses of *kerussein* in the Synoptics deal with
the preaching of the disciples. Mark 3:14 associates the sending out of the Twelve with their appointment. This commission to preach and exorcize is not carried out until 6:7-13,
where, in verse 12, it is recorded that repentance was the burden of their message. This account is given in Luke as his
first mission account (9:1-6).[63] That the preaching of repentance in Mark is given in Luke as "bringing good news"
(9:6) shows that for the writer of the Third Gospel there
was nothing incompatible between these two concepts.

Since the two appearances of *kerussein* in the long ending
of Mark (16:15, 20) are necessarily subsequent to the final
issue of the Jewish-Gentile controversy that culminated in the
Council of Jerusalem (Acts 15), it may be said that this verb
continued as the characteristic expression or the public proclamation of the good news of God's redemptive act.

Let us now note briefly those elements in the preaching of
Jesus and His disciples which may be said to be most characteristic.

The divine commission necessary for all true preaching is
perhaps the most prominent feature. Jesus was *sent* to proclaim spiritual deliverance (Luke 4:18). For this reason He

---

63 The second Lucan mission — that of the 70/72 — (Luke 10:1-16)
seems to be a composite from Q and L. Manson (*Sayings*, pp. 73-74)
says that the mention of the 72 was probably taken from L, and thus
suggested a separate mission. However, it may be that the L reference
is actually a doublet of the mission of the Twelve in the other sources.
No final answer is needed here. The important thing is that this preaching mission is one of the best-attested events in the life of Christ.

THE PREACHING OF JESUS AND THE TWELVE   51

must not linger in any one town, but must push on (Mark 1:38). The disciples are likewise commissioned to go to the house of Israel and proclaim, "The kingdom of heaven is at hand" (Matt. 10:7). They are again sent forth by the risen Lord — this time to carry the Gospel to all the world (Matt. 28:19-20, Mark 16:15). A divine commission is the *sine qua non* of true preaching.

The divine commissioning takes place in view of an urgent situation. Men are "harassed and helpless, like sheep without a shepherd." They desperately need to know that God has at long last engaged the foe in mortal combat and is winning the decisive victory. "The harvest is plentiful, but the laborers are few" (Matt. 9:37). The message *must* be sounded forth.

Finally, the element of repentance plays a significant role in the preaching of Jesus and His disciples. It must not, however, be separated from its true counterpart — Messianic blessedness. Jesus came to bring good news. His message was one of great joy, but this joy was only for those who would turn from their sinfulness. As Jesus' Capernaum ministry was a "great light" for "those who sat in the region and shadow of death" (Matt. 4:16), so also was His Kingdom message a wellspring of joy supernal to those who bowed their hearts in genuine humility.

Chapter Four

PREACHING IN THE EARLY CHURCH

THE concept of heralding cannot be limited to the initial proclamation of the Kingdom. It is the characteristic way throughout the entire New Testament of referring to the ongoing proclamation of the Christ-event. *Kerussein* occurs nine times in Acts alone. Paul uses it in all but three of his epistles. Outside the Gospels, the verb is found twenty-nine times in the New Testament and in all but four it represents the distinctive missionary activity of the early Church. The aim of this chapter is to examine two different aspects of the apostolic preaching: that which is said to have been heralded, and the nature of the heralding itself.

THE MESSAGE PROCLAIMED

When we leave the Synoptics and move out into the rest of the New Testament we discover, in connection with the concept of heralding, a basic change of terminology. The phrase that was so often upon the lips of the Synoptists, "the kingdom of God," has all but completely disappeared. In its place is the preaching of "Christ." This is variously expressed as "Christ crucified" (I Cor. 1:23), "Christ . . . raised" (I Cor. 15:12), "the Son of God, Jesus Christ" (II Cor. 1:19), or "Jesus Christ as Lord" (II Cor. 4:5). It is readily apparent that the central thrust of the apostolic message was not the Kingdom, but the exalted King.

What accounts for this shift? Simply this. "The Gospel of Christ replaced the Gospel of the Kingdom, because by his death he became the kingdom."[1] Christ *is* the Kingdom. To preach Christ is to preach the Kingdom. The Jews had anticipated the time when the sovereign rule of God would be es-

1 P. T. Forsyth, *The Person and Place of Jesus Christ*, p. 122.

tablished over all mankind. Jesus announced the advent of
that rule. In and through Jesus Christ, God was acting redemptively for mankind. "The Kingdom was Christ in a
mystery; Christ was the publication, the establishment of the
Kingdom."2 As God had brought His eternal purpose into
focus in Jesus Christ, so also could the resulting claims now be
presented more definitely. Decision concerning the King was
a more clear-cut message than allegiance to a Kingdom. In
accordance with the advance in redemptive history, the apostolic Church now proclaimed the Christ.

If this equation between Christ and the Kingdom be true,
we should expect to find a certain degree of overlapping or
identification of terms. And that is so. Acts 8:5 reports that
Philip went into Samaria and "proclaimed to them the *Christ*,"
while in verse 12 his message is called the "good news about
the *kingdom of God* and the name of Jesus Christ." At Corinth
Paul spoke boldly about the *"kingdom of God"* (Acts 19:8);
exorcists then tried to imitate his healings by pronouncing the
name of the *"Jesus* whom Paul preaches" (Acts 19:13). The
risen Christ had appeared to His disciples during forty days,
"speaking of the *kingdom of God"* (Acts 1:3); but His final
charge was that they should be witnesses to *Him* (Acts 1:8).

The verb *kerussein* also takes another object in the New Testament — the "gospel." This is stated directly (Gal. 2:2, Col.
1:23, I Thess. 2:9), or represented by an equivalent phrase
(as "the word of faith" in Rom. 10:8, or simply "the word" as
in II Tim. 4:2), or implied by the context (I Cor. 9:27, 15:11,
Rom. 10:14-16). It is but another way of saying that Christ
is preached. The "word of faith" (the Gospel whose subject
is faith) of Romans 10:8 is explained in the following verses
as an acknowledgment of the person of Christ and the truth
of His resurrection. To preach the Gospel is to preach Christ.

In view of the frequency with which we hear the word
kerygma in current theological discussion, we are somewhat
surprised to find that the actual noun (κήρυγμα) occurs but
eight times in the New Testament. C. H. Dodd has emphasized that it signifies "not the action of the preacher, but that

2 *Ibid.*, p. 123.

which he preaches, his 'message.' "[3] In this he is supported
by the majority of lexicographers.[4] However, there are some
who hesitate to accept such a pat definition, feeling that the
activity involved in heralding is very much present in the
word.[5] Hence it will be well to canvass the New Testament
evidence with this question in mind.

We notice first that in some of the verses *kerygma* quite
clearly indicates the content of the proclamation. The *kerygma*
of Jesus Christ in Romans 16:25 is best understood in this way.
So also is the "sacred and indestructible *kerygma*" of the short
ending of Mark. With some hesitation I Corinthians 1:21 may
also be included in this category. By the "folly of what we
preach" (RSV) God saves those who believe. Against the
weight of current opinion Evans suggests that Paul may have
been contrasting two activities: the activity of wisdom by
which the world did not know God, and the activity of preaching by which God saved those who believed. However, as the
syntax of the Greek clearly shows, the antithetical elements are
"wisdom" and "foolishness," not "wisdom" and *"kerygma."*

On the other hand, *kerygma* in at least one place (Titus 1:3)
seems quite definitely to mean activity. It is "through *preaching"* that the word which brings eternal life is manifested.
Preaching is the manner in which the divine word comes to
us — its vehicle of manifestation.

Friedrich takes *kerygma* in II Timothy 4:17 to mean the
preaching office.[6] In verse 5 Paul has admonished Timothy,
"Fulfill your ministry." In verse 7 he writes, "I have
finished the race, I have kept the faith." Finally (says Friedrich) Paul concludes that the Lord had strengthened him that
he could fully carry out his preaching office so that by this

3 *The Apostolic Preaching and Its Developments*, p. 7.

4 Cf. especially Abbott-Smith (*A Manual Greek Lexicon of the New
Testament*), where *kerygma* is said to be "the substance as distinct from
the act, which would be expressed by κήρυξις."

5 C. F. Evans, "The Kerygma," *Journal of Theological Studies*, April
1956, and Donald J. Selby ("The Pre-Literary Development of the Kerygma," unpublished Ph.D. dissertation, Boston University, 1954) in correspondence.

6 In *Theologisches Wörterbuch zum Neuen Testament*, III, 716.

means all the Gentiles might hear. This interpretation, as tempting as it may be, must remain more a possibility than a probability. The very phraseology ("The Lord . . . strengthened me, that through me "the *kerygma*" might be fully carried out") suggests that the *kerygma* was a semi-technical term for the Gospel message, analogous to "the faith" which Paul has kept (v. 7), and "the message" that Alexander opposed (v. 15). Friedrich's conjecture would have more weight if the verse could be shown to be the work of a later hand, and thus perhaps reflect a post-apostolic ecclesiastical development. But, as a matter of fact, even P. N. Harrison includes it as one of the fine genuine notes of Paul.[7] The divine strengthening has been to the end that the proclamation of the Gospel — not Paul's preaching office — might be fully carried out and that all the Gentiles might hear.

In the remaining verses, and perhaps even to a lesser degree in those already discussed, *kerygma* refuses to be stereotyped as an either/or product. Although both emphases are present, it is the content that is usually the dominant element.

Thus we conclude that the term *kerygma* as used in the New Testament has a twofold connotation. In some instances it refers primarily to the content of the message; in others, to the act of proclaiming. At the same time it resists any exclusive label. It is neither subject matter alone nor simply the act of proclaiming. It is the proclamation viewed as a whole. Similar to the Declaration of Independence, it demands an existential, not a static, frame of reference. It is *The Proclamation*.

THE PROCLAIMING OF THE MESSAGE

When we look at the apostolic preaching from the standpoint of activity instead of content, we are able to single out several of its more prominent characteristics.

In the first place, preaching directed to audiences predominantly Jewish had a distinctly polemic quality. Paul at Damascus "confounded the Jews . . . by proving that Jesus was the Christ" (Acts 9:22). In Jerusalem he preached boldly

---

7 P. N. Harrison, *The Problem of the Pastoral Epistles*, p. 121.

and "disputed against the Hellenists" (Acts 9:29). In Thessalonica he "argued with them from the scriptures, explaining and proving that it was necessary for the Christ to suffer and to rise from the dead, and saying, 'This Jesus, whom I proclaim to you, is the Christ' " (Acts 17:2-3). In Corinth (Acts 18:4-5; cf. II Cor. 1:19) and Ephesus (Acts 19:8-9) the story is the same. Near the close of his ministry Paul was still "testifying to the kingdom of God and trying to convince them [the Jews] about Jesus" (Acts 28:23). Thus, when Jewish opposition was encountered, preaching became definitely polemic. To preach involved a dialectical entanglement with the opposition. Mere announcement of historical event would not suffice. Hence, arguing, testifying, pleading, and proving — all were necessary parts of early preaching.

A second noticeable characteristic of New Testament preaching was the divine commission. Romans 10:15 ("How can men preach unless they are sent?") is absolutely crucial for the understanding of the preaching office. Without a commission, the preaching of Christ is only propaganda. In fact, we may say that apart from a commission, there can exist no preaching at all in the true sense of the word.

Apostolic preaching everywhere reveals its consciousness of a divine commission. In his kerygmatic summary to the household of Cornelius, Peter relates that the risen Lord had *commanded* them to preach to the people (Acts 10:42). This sense of having been divinely commissioned is especially noticeable in Paul. God had chosen him for a special purpose (Acts 9:15). He preached not of his own will but as one "entrusted with a commission" (I Cor. 9:17). This commission was not concerned with peripheral issues such as baptism (I Cor. 1:17), but with the preaching of an entrusted Gospel (Gal. 2:2, I Thess. 2:4). "God has trusted me to tell men about his offer to forgive and accept them" is Laubach's straightforward translation of II Corinthians 5:19.[8] Although the commission to preach originated with God (II Cor. 1:21), it could be supplemented with guidance by the Spirit (Acts 11:12) and encouraged through subsequent visions (Acts 18:9-10).

God's command creates an urgent situation. Preaching is not a relaxed recital of interesting but morally neutral events. "Woe to me if I do not preach the gospel!" exclaimed Paul (I Cor. 9:16). God had commissioned him, and completely apart from what he might want to do, he had to preach. This inner compulsion made him carry on in spite of disbelief, opposition, and danger to life. Paul says that in Ephesus he served the Lord "with all humility and with tears and with trials" (Acts 20:19). Why? Because he was under divine commission. Anything less than a whole-soul abandonment to the expressed will of God would be treason.

What was true of Paul was also true of the entire apostolic Church. Although persecuted and driven from Jerusalem, they answered the threat of imprisonment by going about "preaching the word" (Acts 8:4). "Preach the word, be urgent in season and out of season" was the advice given to Timothy (II Tim. 4:2).

Bringing men to grips with the issues of eternity is no passive enterprise. It is through the message proclaimed by the herald that the Word of God invades man's moral realm and demands decision. Opposition to this divine intervention often takes the form of opposition to the one who bears the message. Thus the apostolic herald lived no life of comfort and prestige in a sheltered parish. "Endure suffering" was the charge given to Timothy by one who had experienced a full share of opposition, affliction (II Cor. 4:8-12), and just plain hard work (cf. I Cor. 15:10, I Thess. 2:9).

Over against these hardships, which were mostly external, there was another type of opposition. This was the subtle temptation somehow to avoid the stigma that came from espousing a socially objectionable cause. To the Jews, the Cross was a stumbling block. To the Greeks, it was folly. How inviting to alter the message just enough to rid it of its objectionable quality. But the herald is forbidden to tamper with the proclamation. He must resist the constant pressure to conform. As a result he is harassed from every quarter; persecuted from without, tempted from within.

A third feature of apostolic preaching was its transparency of message and motive. Since the *kerygma* demands faith,

it is absolutely imperative that the issues be not obscured by
eloquent wisdom and lofty words. Clarity at any cost is the
keynote. The naked truth is self-authenticating. To prop
it up with eloquence or philosophy is to rob it of its power
(I Cor. 1:17). Paul insisted that he had renounced "disgrace-
ful underhanded ways" — that he had refused "to practice
cunning or to tamper with God's word." Rather, he would
commend himself to every man's conscience by "the open statement of the truth" (II Cor. 4:2). The true herald aims to
please God, not man (I Thess. 2:4). Devices for personal
gain, such as flattery, are completely out of place (I Thess.
2:5).

This transparency must be maintained because of the paradoxical nature of the message. From the prevailing Jewish
point of view, a crucified Christ was too great an obstacle to
surmount. As for the Greeks, to them it was sheer folly (I
Cor. 1:22-23). How then can the message break through?
Only by a radical upheaval within the heart and consciousness
of the one who hears. This does not come about by the persuasive influence of rhetoric or by a toning down of the
"folly" of the message, but by the new insight of faith. It
is to those who believe that Christ is both "the power of God
and the wisdom of God" (I Cor. 1:24). Such faith arises most
readily when the Gospel is proclaimed with simplicity of expression in an atmosphere of transparency of motive.

How did people react to this kind of preaching? One thing
is certain — they could not remain neutral. Wherever the
apostolic *kerygma* was proclaimed there was either a "revival
or a riot." At the very outset of Paul's career as a herald
his preaching drove a wedge into the populace of Damascus.
While some were closing in with the intent to kill, others were
risking their lives by lowering him over the wall to safety (Acts
9:23-25). At Thessalonica, where Paul proclaimed Jesus to
be the Christ (Acts 17:3), some were persuaded but others
stormed the house of Jason in a frantic effort to get their
hands on those who had "turned the world upside down"
(v. 6). Everywhere Paul carried the Gospel, the reaction was
the same. Some believed, while others violently rebelled. It
was impossible to remain neutral when faced with the claims

of a risen Christ. Opposition to the message resulted in antagonism toward the messenger. Where the proclamation was received there was much joy (Acts 8:8). Where it was rejected there was opposition and bitter hatred.

These, then, are the most prominent features of the apostolic preaching. To audiences predominantly Jewish, preaching was decidedly polemic. It involved proving that the historic Jesus was both Son of God and exalted Lord. Man did not enter into this ministry of his own volition. Only those called and commissioned by God were authentic heralds. Without a commission there could be no true preaching. God's command created an urgent situation. This urgency ruled out all complacency. Because the message was a life-and-death matter, the herald *must* proclaim. This inner compulsion drove him on in face of opposition and hardship. Neither danger to life nor temptation to conform must alter his message. He was to preach Christ with crystal clarity and transparency of life.

Chapter Five

THE APOSTOLIC PROCLAMATION

IT is inevitable that any fresh study of the apostolic preaching will take as its point of departure the work of C. H. Dodd in *The Apostolic Preaching and Its Developments* (1936). His crystallization of the primitive *kerygma* has rightly been hailed as "one of the most important and positive contributions to New Testament science in our generation."[1]

C. H. DODD AND THE KERYGMA

Professor Dodd begins his task by examining the fragments of early Christian tradition embedded in the Pauline epistles. This tradition was received by Paul not more than seven years after the crucifixion. It may therefore be taken as relatively primitive. From this material there emerges the outlines of an apostolic Gospel:

> The prophecies are fulfilled, and the New Age is inaugurated by the coming of Christ.
> He was born of the seed of David.
> He died according to the Scriptures, to deliver us out of the present evil age.
> He was buried.
> He rose on the third day according to the Scriptures.
> He is exalted at the right hand of God, as Son of God and Lord of quick and dead.
> He will come again as Judge and Savior of men.[2]

A second source of evidence (less direct, but of great importance) is supplied by the early speeches in Acts. These are not free compositions of Luke — the figment of an historian's imagination — but rest upon early material that proceeded from the Aramaic-speaking church at Jerusalem. A

---

1 A. M. Hunter, *The Unity of the New Testament*, p. 22.
2 C. H. Dodd, *The Apostolic Preaching*, p. 17.

survey of the speeches in Acts 2, 3, 4, and 10 yields the following summary:

The age of fulfillment has dawned.

This has taken place through the ministry, death, and resurrection of Jesus.

By virtue of the resurrection, Jesus has been exalted at the right hand of God, as Messianic head of the new Israel.

The Holy Spirit in the Church is the sign of Christ's present power and glory.

The Messianic Age will shortly reach its consummation in the return of Christ.

An appeal for repentance.[3]

When these two summaries are compared, they are found to cover essentially the same ground. Any divergencies can be explained. This remarkable correspondence allows us to carry back the essential elements of the speeches in Acts to a date far earlier than a critical analysis of the book by itself would justify. The resultant *kerygma* is defined as "a proclamation of the death and resurrection of Jesus Christ, in an eschatological setting from which those facts derive their saving significance."[4]

RETHINKING THE KERYGMA

Not all have agreed with Dodd at every point. Some have objected to his acceptance of the speeches in Acts as valid evidence for apostolic preaching.[5] Others would alter the items included in the *kerygma*.[6] The most common objection, however, has to do with the general impression that is created by his formulation. The impression created that the *kerygma* is a sort of stereotyped six-headed sermon which the apostles delivered on any and every occasion. Paul Davies writes, "I confess that Dodd's *kerygma* leaves me with a feeling

3 *Ibid.*, pp. 21-24.

4 *Ibid.*, p. 24. Note the definition on p. 13 as well.

5 H. J. Cadbury, "Acts and Eschatology," *The Background of the New Testament and Its Eschatology*, p. 317; C. F. Evans, "The Kerygma," *Journal of Theological Studies*, VII (April 1956), 25-41.

6 T. F. Glasson, "The Kerygma: Is Our Version Correct?" *The Hibbert Journal*, LI (Jan. 1953), 129-32.

of having been robbed of the fulness of Christ in the interests
of a unified formula, although at the same time I would accept
his conclusions."[7] G. B. Caird senses this danger and would
guard against it by reminding us that the message "was delivered with a warmth of enthusiastic conviction by men who had
experienced the blessings they proclaimed."[8] William Baird
would explain Dodd's "factual *kerygma*" (as over against
Bultmann's "dynamic") as a result of defining it in terms of
form rather than content.[9] While all these observations are
true, they overlook a more basic point which is that the individual apostolic sermon (at least as it is reproduced in Acts)
does not fit the outline of Dodd's reconstructed *kerygma*.

This assertion needs to be validated. Let us examine, by
way of example, Peter's speech on the day of Pentecost (Acts
2:14-36). Observe closely the movement of thought.

Peter begins by informing the perplexed multitude that the
speaking in tongues was not the result of too much wine. It
was much too early in the day for that. Rather, it was the
fulfillment of the ancient prophecy that in the last days God
would pour out His Spirit, causing young and old to prophesy,
dream dreams, and see visions.

He then turns to the historic Jesus of Nazareth, and in a
converging line of argumentation shows the relationship of
Jesus to the present phenomenon. His point of departure is
the divine attestation of Jesus by means of mighty works, wonders, and signs. This basic premise they granted, for these
things had taken place in their very midst. A second point
they could not deny was that as a people they had lawlessly
crucified Him.

These two points set the stage for Peter's central thrust —
the resurrection. It was impossible that the bonds of death
should hold Him. Why? Because in passages like Psalm
16:8-11 His resurrection had been prophesied. But could
not this prediction refer to David himself? Hardly, in view

7 Paul Davies, "Unity and Variety in the New Testament," *Interpretation*, V (April 1951), 182.

8 G. B. Caird, *The Apostolic Age*, p. 38.

9 William Baird, "What Is the Kerygma?" *Journal of Biblical Literature*, LXXVI (Sept. 1957), 181-91.

of the fact that he had died, was buried, and his tomb was still intact.   It follows that the prophecy must refer to the resurrection of the Messianic King, of whom David was but a figure. Who only has been raised?   Jesus — and we are witnesses of this.   Therefore, Jesus of Nazareth is God's Messiah.

As Messiah He was exalted at God's right hand.   Exaltation involves reception of the promised Holy Spirit.   This Spirit has now been poured out (as Jesus promised) and this accounts for the supernatural display.

In explaining the outpouring of the Spirit, Peter also had proved the Messiahship of Jesus by virtue of the resurrection. Taking this as a pivotal point, he now directs the argument to an evangelistic climax.   By showing that the Lordly exaltation of Psalm 110 could not refer to David (since it was not he that ascended), but rather to the One who did ascend, he emphasizes a further role of the risen Jesus.   The One they had crucified, God made not only Christ, but also Lord.

Is it any wonder that they were cut to the heart and cried, "Brethren, what shall we do?"   To have laid violent hands on God's Annointed was unspeakable blasphemy.   There was but one answer: "Repent, and be baptized . . . in the name of Jesus Christ."   This would result in forgiveness and the gift of the Holy Spirit.

It should be evident by now that this sermon does not follow the lines of the standard *kerygma*.[10]   Far from being a formal proclamation of the dawn of a New Age — how it came about and its results — it is an extemporaneous explanation of an unusual phenomenon.   Its purpose is to confront men with the inescapable fact that the very One they had crucified, God had made both Lord and Christ.   Peter is much more concerned to bring into focus man's responsibility than he is to explain the theological implications of the Messiah's advent.   Thus, while the Pentecost speech is composed of the same general

10 Martin Dibelius ("The Speeches in Acts and Ancient Historiography," *Studies in the Acts of the Apostles*, pp. 165-66) strangely enough finds in the speeches a stereotyped repetition of the same outline.   He even goes so far as to raise the question as to whether this outline might not have existed in written form.

raw materials as the standard *kerygma* formula, the finished product is strikingly different.

When the other speeches in Acts are examined in respect to form, they also are found to bear only a passing resemblance to the accepted *kerygma*. How are we to account for this?

The crux of the trouble lies in a misunderstanding of what the *kerygma* is meant to represent. It is not the outline of any particular sermon. Much less is it a ready-made proclamation that was delivered on every occasion by all the apostles alike. Rather, it represents the apostolic message in a much wider sense. It is a systematic statement of the theology of the primitive Church as revealed in the early preaching. As such, it is not a sermon with so many heads, but a survey of primitive Christology conveniently arranged as such.

This observation should make us less critical of the cut-and-dried flavor of kerygmatic studies. At the same time, it shows that for a true view of the apostolic message, we must not approach it as if it were content only. Lexicographical study led us to conclude that κήρυγμα, as used in the New Testament, does not mean content only, but content in the act of being proclaimed.[11] To be rightly understood it must be seen in an existential, not static, frame of reference. It is imperative that the apostolic preaching be studied as a living thing. We must be caught up by the message as it is being proclaimed, irresistibly carried along by its progression of thought, and we must actually experience its moral implications. Otherwise our reconstruction will lack that vital dimension called life.

For this reason I propose to begin the study of the *kerygma* with the speeches in Acts. Here we can recapture something of that primitive atmosphere. To search for the essence of apostolic preaching by a statistical evaluation of the content is like dissecting a corpse to find the principle of life. Methodology has excluded the answer before the quest has begun.

After the speeches in Acts have been reviewed in context, we can then crystallize their comprehensive message — the *kerygma* in its widest sense. This procedure will bring to light

11 Cf. above, pp. 53-55.

the reasons for contesting one of the major emphases in Dodd's reconstruction. It will also necessitate a few changes in the actual content of the accepted *kerygma*.

TWO BASIC QUESTIONS

Before beginning this, however, there are two preliminary questions that must be answered. The first is, Which of the some twenty speeches in Acts give valid evidence of the primitive *kerygma*? What is our justification for accepting some while excluding others?

(1) *Which speeches are truly primitive?*

If preaching be defined as "the public proclamation of Christianity to the non-Christian world,"[12] then it is readily apparent that certain of the speeches in Acts will fall outside our present inquiry. Peter's speech in which he recommends that another witness to the resurrection be chosen (1:16-22), or Paul's farewell address to the Ephesian elders (20:18-35), may throw light on early Christian thought, but they are not directly involved in the public proclamation of Christianity. It is the missionary or evangelistic speeches in Acts that give firsthand evidence of the primitive *kerygma*.

There is little difficulty in determining which of the speeches in Acts are evangelistic. With F. F. Bruce[13] we would include in this category the early Petrine speeches (2-5, 10) and those of Paul in chapters 13, 14, and 17.

But are all of these eight speeches of one stratum? Are they all equally primitive? Hardly so. While the early Petrine speeches (2-5) represent the first flush of Christianity (on, or shortly after, the year A.D. 30), Paul's speeches are clustered around a mid-century date.

This lapse of some fifteen to twenty years is by itself suffi-

12 Dodd, *op. cit.*, p. 7.
13 F. F. Bruce, *The Speeches in the Acts of the Apostles*, p. 5. Bo Reicke ("A Synopsis of Early Christian Preaching," *The Root of the Vine*, pp. 128-160) singles out the same speeches and classifies them under the heading, "Conversion." Bruce designates the other speeches as Deliberative (1, 15), Apologetic (7, 11, 22, 23, 24, 25, 26, 28), and Hortatory (20).

cient ground for excluding Paul's speeches as primary evidence. There are other reasons as well. His Athenian address (17:22-31) and his words at Lystra (14:15-17) are not to be taken as typical examples of evangelistic preaching. At Athens Paul attempts an "unparalleled conciliatory approach."[14] When he arrived at his real message — the risen Christ — he lost his audience. At Lystra, Paul and Barnabas are engaged in restraining a mob from offering sacrifice to them. What they happen to say in such a crucial situation can in no wise be construed as a typical sermon.

Paul's speech at Antioch of Pisidia (13:16-41) must also be excluded as primary evidence. The fourteen or fifteen years that have elapsed since Pentecost have allowed a certain amount of theological reflection and development. Commenting on verse 39 and its reference to "justification," Lake and Cadbury cannot "resist the belief that this verse is an attempt to express Pauline doctrine."[15] While this judgment may go a bit beyond the evidence, it is a realistic attempt to account for certain indications of a developing theological outlook. More probable is Bruce's opinion that the Antioch speech represents a natural transition from the primitive preaching of the early chapters of Acts to the more mature doctrine found in the epistles.[16]

But what of Peter's speech in Acts 10? Does it breathe the same atmosphere as the early speeches or does it represent a later phase? The events of chapters 6-9 would suggest that a considerable span of time had intervened. However, internal evidence leads to a different conclusion.

Peter appeals to his listeners' knowledge of Jesus in respect to His Galilean ministry — how He was anointed with the Spirit and power, and went about doing good. Yet, there was something else that they did not know. This was that Jesus had been put to death, then raised by God and exalted to be Judge of the living and the dead. From this lack of informa-

---

14 Floyd V. Filson, *Jesus Christ the Risen Lord*, p. 40.
15 *The Beginnings of Christianity*, IV, 157.
16 Bruce, *The Acts of the Apostles*, p. 272.

tion it would appear that the Cornelius episode followed close upon the day of Pentecost.[17]

Why, then, is it placed in Acts at what seems to be a later date? This is undoubtedly due to Luke's scheme of composition. In harmony with the expanding witness of Acts 1:8 (Jerusalem, Judea, Samaria, ends of the earth) it is placed at this point because of its pivotal significance. There are no time indications that demand that the material be taken in strict chronological sequence. W. L. Knox notes, "There is no reason to suppose that the sermon has any organic connection with its present context; it is simply a specimen of the primitive preaching included here because the occasion seemed suitable."[18]

Since the Cornelius speech need not be placed at a later date so as to allow for the intervening events of chapters 6-9, and since its internal evidence points to a time before Caesarea knew of the death and resurrection of the Prophet of Galilee, we accept this speech along with those in Acts 2-5 as providing the proper source material for the primitive *kerygma*.

(2) Are the speeches in Acts reliable?

But now a second and more basic question arises. How may we be sure that these speeches represent the gist of what was actually said? Is it not possible that they are free compositions of Luke — figments of his historical imagination?

This question has been warmly debated. While Dodd accepts the speeches as based on early material proceeding from the Aramaic-speaking church at Jerusalem,[19] Cadbury maintains that they are "devoid of historical basis in genuine tradition."[20] Knox believes that there is every reason to regard

17 F. J. Foakes-Jackson (*The Acts of the Apostles*, p. 94) concludes that the events recorded in the early chapters of Acts (including the baptism of Cornelius) happened within an astonishingly brief period.

18 W. L. Knox, *The Acts of the Apostles*, p. 31.

19 Dodd, *The Apostolic Preaching*, p. 20.

20 Cadbury, "The Speeches in Acts," *The Beginnings of Christianity*, V, 426. It should be added, however, that Cadbury sees in them a certain historical value. They are what a well-informed Christian of the next generation thought might have been the main outline of the original message.

their picture of the primitive faith as reliable,[21] but Dibelius concludes that as they stand they are "inventions of the author."[22] Since this question is crucial for the determination of the *kerygma*, it must be dealt with in some fullness.

It may safely be assumed that Luke stood in the general tradition of Greek historiography. The principles and methods employed by all ancient historians were his as well. In connection with the recording of speeches, the ideal method is best described by Thucydides in his preface to the *History of the Peloponnesian War*. Here he explains that since it was impossible to carry the speeches word for word in his memory, it was his habit to make the speakers say what in his opinion the various occasions demanded of them. He safeguards this statement by adding, "of course adhering as closely as possible to the general sense of what they really said."[23]

Unfortunately, this statement has been misconstrued to mean that "from Thucydides downwards, speeches reported by the historians are confessedly pure imagination."[24] This is not a valid inference. It ultimately leads to an unfair estimate of the historical value of the Lukan material. What Thucydides is actually doing is repudiating verbal exactitude in the interests of true history. His honest admission that he cannot reproduce the *ipsissima verba* of the speeches is certainly no indication that what he does write is "pure imagination." There is no reason to doubt that Thucydides conscientiously accomplished what he set out to do.

If all subsequent historians had inherited Thucydides' historical conscience, there would have been no question about the speeches in Acts. But they did not. The historical speech became a device to exhibit the dramatic and rhetorical skill of the historian. Writers like Josephus placed an oratorical eloquence in the mouths of their characters that would have com-

---

21 Knox, *op. cit.*, p. 68.

22 Dibelius, *A Fresh Approach to the New Testament and Early Christian Literature*, p. 262. Cf. also *The Message of Jesus*, pp. 129ff.

23 *History of the Peloponnesian War*, i. 22 (I. R. Crawley's translation).

24 H. J. Cadbury, "The Greek and Jewish Traditions of Writing History," *Beginnings*, II, 13.

pletely dumbfounded those who supposedly spoke the words.[25] Dionysius of Halicarnasses alludes to the common belief that the summit of a writer's genius lies in his ability to compose eloquent speeches.[26]

But what do we find when we look at the speeches in Acts? Far from being the summit of Luke's literary ability, they are written in a style of Greek that is often awkward, and at times untranslatable. By no stretch of the imagination can these speeches be thought to represent Luke at his best. Nor do they reflect any of the artificial grandeur of an uncontrolled imagination. As a writer of historical speeches, Luke is certainly much closer to the conscientious restraint of Thucydides than to the exuberant creativeness of his contemporary, Josephus.

The general trustworthiness of Luke is also attested by his careful use of sources in the Third Gospel. When the speeches there are compared with their Synoptic parallels, it is found that Luke has preserved his Sayings' source with great faithfulness. To be sure, there are changes, but these are stylistic and do not materially affect the content. F. C. Burkitt compares the Eschatological Discourse in Luke 21 with its earlier form in Mark 13 and concludes that although there are differences, "what concerns us here is not that Luke has changed so much, but that he has invented so little."[27] Is it not probable that Luke maintained this same literary fidelity in his second book?

When we examine the speeches themselves, there are several important strands of evidence that strengthen the case for their historical validity. First, they have a strong Semitic coloring. Wherever we turn, we constantly meet indications of an Aramaic background. These Semitisms, which lurk in almost every verse, are not Hebraisms (which could be accounted for by the influence of the LXX), but are genuine Aramaisms. While Torrey's theory that Acts 1-15 represents Luke's translation of

25 Cf. the speech he assigns to Abraham when he is on the point of sacrificing Isaac (Antiquities of the Jews, i. 13. 3).

26 De Thucydide, 34.

27 F. C. Burkitt, "The Use of Mark in the Essays According to Luke," Beginnings, II, 115.

a single Aramaic document has not found general acceptance, the strong evidence for Aramaisms in 1:1b-5:16 and 9:31-11:18 cannot be denied.[28] The only explanation for this phenomenon is that behind the speeches, as we have them in the Greek text of Acts, lies some form of Aramaic sources.

This becomes even more probable when we consider that certain sections that are meaningless as they stand in Greek, become both grammatical and intelligible when put back into Aramaic. A literal translation of Acts 3:16 reads, "In the faith in His name, His name hath strengthened this man whom ye see and know and the faith that is through Him hath given him this health." The Aramaic substratum, with a slightly different pointing, yields, "And through faith in His name, He has made whole this man whom you see and know. . . ."[29]

Peter's speech to the household of Cornelius (Acts 10) also presents a strong case for an Aramaic original.[30] This is especially significant, because here, more than in any other speech, we would have expected Peter to speak Greek. What we have, however, is a text that, unless one resorts to desperate emendations, almost defies translation. Retranslated into Aramaic, it makes perfectly good sense. It follows that Luke was either "wrestling here with an intractable Aramaic source"[31] or incorporating an already translated account. If he were doing the latter, then his reluctance to tamper with the linguistic and grammatical peculiarities would suggest that he did not wish to alter in any way this original version of the primitive Gospel.

28 Cf. J. De Zwaan, "The Use of the Greek Language in Acts," *Beginnings*, II, 44-61.

29 Torrey, *op. cit.*, pp. 14ff.

30 C. F. Evans ("The Kerygma," *Journal of Theological Studies*, VII [April 1956], 25-41) takes Acts 10:34-43 as an example of a speech that is so predominantly Lukan in style and subject matter that "there seems little room left for an aramaic original" (p. 38). However, the Lukan characteristics (Evans' comparisons are somewhat overdrawn) can be explained on the basis that Luke most certainly edited the speeches. But how, from Evans' point of view, can the undeniable Aramaisms be accounted for? His entire article raises many such doubts, and falls short in not giving an adequate explanation for the positive data.

31 Hunter, *The Unity of the New Testament*, p. 23.

In any event, such evidence makes it difficult to resist the conclusion that the early speeches in Acts first existed in an Aramaic source or sources. This, of course, greatly enhances their historical respectability.

That sources were available to Luke should not take us by surprise. There is good reason to believe that Luke conceived of the Gospel and the Acts as constituting one single work.[32] As such, the method and purpose set forth in the Prologue (Luke 1:1-4) would refer to both sections. Here we find that *many others* had undertaken to compile similar narratives. While the work of Luke's predecessors was undoubtedly centered on the life, death, and resurrection of Christ, the possibility cannot be excluded that some may well have dealt with certain aspects of the supernatural founding and early growth of the Church.

Dodd maintains that it is only on the hypothesis of various sources that the three accounts of Paul's conversion can be reasonably explained.[33] Certainly the Pauline traits that are found throughout his speech to the Ephesian Elders (Acts 20: 18-35) indicate that Luke was either using a source or writing from personal recollections.[34] The strange verdict of "pure imagination" is quite untenable.

Let us now consider a second strand of internal evidence. Upon inspection it is found that the early speeches are completely free of any traces of distinctive Pauline theology,[35] and

32 N. B. Stonehouse (*The Witness of Luke to Christ*, pp. 10-13, 24-25) convincingly supports this position. Cf. especially p. 33, where he argues that the things of which Theophilus had been informed can hardly be limited to pre-Ascension events. Certainly the "momentous happenings after the departure of Christ," which were of "decisive significance for the spread of Christianity," called for explanation. Cf. also J. Klausner, *From Jesus to Paul*, p. 218.

33 Dodd, *op. cit.*, p. 18.

34 Percy Gardner ("The Speeches of St. Paul in Acts," *Cambridge Biblical Essays*, pp. 401-04) contends that Luke was present and that emotion fixed the speech in his memory.

35 Dodd (*op. cit.*, p. 19n.) points out that this is not true of the writing in which they are embedded.

they do not contain any ideas or expressions that would cause us to suspect a late and Gentile origin. This would be most remarkable if Luke (a Gentile of the Pauline wing of the Church) had freely invented the speeches in retrospect. Even if we could assign to Luke the motives and ability to write in a deliberately archaic style (a modern innovation at that), it would be almost impossible to believe that he could have done it with such flawless perfection. The naive and primitive atmosphere of the speeches attests their validity.

This argument is strengthened by at least two positive considerations. First, in the earliest speeches in Acts, Jesus is spoken of as the *Pais Theou* (3:17, 26, 4:27, 30). This designation never again appears in Acts or the rest of the New Testament (apart from the citation of Isa. 42:1-4 in Matt. 12:18-21). It is primitive and reflects an early stage of Christian thinking.[36] Jesus had interpreted His own ministry in terms of the Isaianic Servant (Luke 22:37). Would it not be most natural for this interpretation and title to have been carried over into the earliest preaching? As the message moved out onto Gentile soil *Pais Theou* became less meaningful and other designations, such as *Kurios*, came to the front.

Secondly, the earliest speeches envisioned the national repentance of Israel as a practical possibility. In Acts 2:36 the proclamation is directed towards "all the house of Israel." In the following speech Peter excuses their ignorance and urges them to repent so that the Christ might return and bring to them times of Messianic refreshing (3:17-21).

This situation was soon to pass away. Priestly opposition arose (Acts 4:1ff.), and before long developed into a persecution that scattered the Church. By the middle of the century it was held that at last God's wrath had descended upon the Jews (I Thess. 2:14-16). The hope for national repentance reflects an early stage in Christian preaching, and its inclusion

36 Cf. Jeremias, παῖς θεοῦ, in *Theologisches Wörterbuch zum Neuen Testament*, V, 698ff.; V. Taylor, *The Names of Jesus*, pp. 36-37; A. E. J. Rawlinson, *The New Testament Doctrine of the Christ*, pp. 238-41; A. Harnack, *The Date of the Acts and of the Synoptic Gospels*, pp. 106-07.

in the earliest Petrine speeches attests their historical validity.[37] For these reasons — (1) the marked dissimilarity to the imaginative speeches of the Greek historians, (2) the fidelity of Luke to his sources in the Gospel, (3) the strong evidence for Aramaic sources, and (4) the notable lack of Paulinism, coupled with other indications of primitiveness — we conclude that while the early speeches in Acts are not verbatim reports, they nevertheless are faithful summaries of what was actually said. Since they are condensed accounts that reliably give the gist of the original speeches, we may with confidence use them in the reconstruction of the apostolic *kerygma*.

THE PREACHING OF PETER

Let us now return to the speeches themselves. It is important that they be reviewed in context so as to set the stage for our final conclusions. We begin here with Peter's second speech, the one occasioned by the healing of the lame man at the Beautiful Gate (Acts 3:12-26).

The astonishment of the crowd upon seeing the lame man walk and leap leads Peter to assert that such a healing should not cause wonder. Much less should anyone imagine that it had been done by the disciples' power. Whose power was it then? It was the power of the risen and glorified Jesus. The Jews had delivered Him up and denied Him before a reluctant Pilate. Jesus was the Holy and Righteous One — the Author of life — and they had killed Him. But God raised Him, and this resurrection was established by witnesses. It was through the resurrection that God had glorified His Servant. He continues to glorify Him by demonstrating the power of His name. Faith in His name has effected this astonishing cure.

Then Peter directs his speech into a lengthy plea for repentance. Although the "men of Israel" were morally responsible for the death of God's Servant, there were extenuat-

37 W. Manson (*Jesus the Messiah*, pp. 33-34) sees another indication of primitiveness in the accreditation of Jesus the Messiah by external signs (Acts 2:22, 10:38). The Hebrew-Jewish concept of divine revelation in history is one in which God makes Himself known by mighty acts.

ing circumstances. They had acted in ignorance. The sufferings of Christ had been foretold and must needs be fulfilled. Therefore there was yet time to repent and turn to Him. Such a repentance would result in forgiveness of sins and times of refreshing.[38] It would bring about the return of Jesus, who had been appointed Messiah for them.

But, if Jesus is the Messiah, what is hindering the establishment of the final and glorious Kingdom? The time for the final fulfillment of all that God prophesied through His prophets is not yet, and the Messiah will remain in heaven until that time. But he was here as the Prophet like unto Moses. He established His covenant and demands obedience. These intervening days were also foretold by the prophets.

Then Peter makes one final plea. You are the sons of the prophets, the rightful heirs. It is through your posterity that the families of the earth shall be blessed. God has kept His promise. He raised up[39] His Servant. The offer is first of all to you. . . .

But Peter never finished his speech. The priests and Sadducees became annoyed at the proclamation of the resurrection of Jesus and placed Peter and John under arrest for further questioning.

Peter's next recorded speech takes place on the following day (4:8-12, 19b-20). He stands before the religious leaders to answer their scornful[40] question concerning the power by which he had wrought the cure.

Peter, filled with the Spirit, boldly declares that the cripple has been healed by the name of Jesus Christ of Nazareth — that is, by the power contained in the revelation of Jesus of Nazareth as the Messiah. Then he quickly moves on to emphasize fearlessly his accusers' responsibility for the death of Jesus. They had acted in direct opposition to God; they crucified

---

38 Since ἀνάψυξις in Hellenistic Greek means "rest" or "respite," the phrase could possibly mean "a temporary relief attainable through faith." It seems preferable, however, to relate it to the final restoration connected with the return of the Messiah.

39 The reference is not to the resurrection, but to the raising up to a public ministry.

40 The syntax of 4:7 suggests the paraphrase "someone like *you*."

Jesus, but God raised Him from the dead. They had rejected the Stone which God exalted to be the head of the corner. The name of Jesus bears a unique significance in the salvation of man. There is no other name that can accomplish spiritual restoration.

That a notable sign had been performed could not be denied. The cripple, now walking, was irrefutable proof. So the Sanhedrin dismissed Peter and John with the command to speak no longer in the name of Jesus.

This, of course, was an impossible command. It would have meant obeying man rather than God. Thus the apostles continued to preach. This led to another imprisonment and the demand to give an answer for their utter disregard of the Sanhedrin's charge.

Why had they done it? Because God, not man, must be obeyed.[41] The accused now turn on the accusers and charge them with the crucifixion of Jesus. The folly of their action is seen in the fact that God raised and exalted to His right hand the very One they crucified. As leader and Savior He would now turn Israel to repentance and grant them the forgiveness of sins. Peter and the apostles are witnesses to these things. So also is the Holy Spirit whom God gives to those who obey.

The Council is enraged[42] at these bold accusations. They are restrained from violent action only by the sage advice of Gamaliel. Released after a beating and a new charge not to speak of Jesus, they go on their way rejoicing at the honor of suffering for the name.

The final speech to be taken into consideration is that of Peter to the household of Cornelius (Acts 10:34-43). It falls into two parts: a response to the situation, and a presentation of the message.[43] Peter had learned from the experience there that God shows no partiality. Men of every nation — Jew or Gentile — may be acceptable to God. He then reminds his

41 This leads into Peter's fourth speech (Acts 5:29b-32).

42 The truth of the accusations is seen in their penetrating effect (Acts 5:33). The literal meaning of διαπρίω (enrage) is "to saw through."

43 Acts 11:15 suggests that Peter was just getting under way when the Holy Spirit fell. That which is recorded is only part of what Peter intended to say.

audience that they already know much about the Prophet, Jesus of Nazareth. How that God had anointed Him with the Holy Spirit and with power. How that He had gone about doing good and healing those oppressed by the devil.

But the good news of peace was not Israel's private possession. Since Christ was Lord of all, His message was meant for all mankind. They should also be told that this Jesus had been crucified, and that God had raised Him on the third day. The resurrected Christ did not appear openly to all, but only to those who had been chosen as witnesses. But perhaps the risen Christ was only an apparition? Not so; we ate and drank with Him.

Peter then relates the command that they should preach and testify that Jesus is the one ordained to be Judge of the living and the dead. All the prophets have borne witness to Him, and all who believe in Him will receive forgiveness of sins.

While Peter was still talking, the Holy Spirit fell on those assembled and they began to speak in tongues. Since the Gentiles also received the Spirit, there was no reason why they should not be baptized. And they were.

THE APOSTOLIC KERYGMA

Having reviewed the speeches in Acts, we are now in a position to bring into focus their essential message. It will be remembered that the *kerygma* is not to be thought of as a standard apostolic sermon, delivered on any and every occasion. It is, rather, a systematic statement of the theology of the early Church arranged as such. Now it is of the utmost importance that the major divisions of its reconstruction represent, at the same time, the logical structure of any individual speech. For if this is not so, the resultant shift of emphasis would fatally obscure the authentic thrust of the original message.

Therefore, a valid reconstruction requires two things: on the one hand, statistical accuracy, and on the other, a sympathetic understanding of the purpose and movement of thought in each speech. The first guarantees that minor points do not appear as major considerations; the second, that the results of statistical inquiry are not interpreted on a dead-level basis but with a proper appreciation of their varying degrees of significance.

With these governing principles in mind, we suggest that the *kerygma,* in simplest outline, would contain:

(1) A proclamation of the death, resurrection, and exaltation of Jesus, seen as the fulfillment of prophecy and involving man's responsibility.

(2) The resultant evaluation of Jesus as both Lord and Christ.

(3) A summons to repent and receive forgiveness of sins.

Let us now develop the total message under these heads.

(1) *The historical proclamation*

(a) *The death*

The death of Jesus is absolutely basic to the apostolic *kerygma.* Historically speaking, it is the first of the three great foundation stones upon which the early Church erected its evangelistic ministry.

This death was not accidental. It was according to the definite plan and foreknowledge of God (2:23) and in fulfillment of what God had foretold through the prophets (3:18). Instead of choosing the Holy and Righteous One, the Jews denied Him before Pilate (3:13) and chose rather a murderer (3:14). In this they rejected the very Stone that was made head of the corner (4:11).

The death of Jesus was particularly degrading because as a common criminal He was hanged on a tree (5:30, 10:39).[44] Although the vile deed was carried out by the hands of lawless men (2:23), the Jewish nation — especially the religious leaders — were morally responsible (2:23, 36, 3:15, 4:10, 5:30, 10:39).

The personal responsibility of the Jews is the strongest feature in the presentation of the death of Jesus. In every speech

44 The feelings of the Romans about crucifixion are expressed by Cicero (*The Second Speech Against Gaius Verres,* v. 66) — "To bind a Roman citizen is a crime, to flog him is an abomination, to slay him is almost an act of murder: to crucify him is — what? There is no fitting word that can possibly describe so horrible a deed" (L. H. G. Greenwood's translation, *Loeb Classical Library*). For the Jewish view, cf. Deut. 21:23.

(except the one to the household of Cornelius — a Gentile audience) Peter boldly declares their involvement in the guilt. So bold were his accusations that the Sanhedrin charged him with filling all Jerusalem with his teaching and intending to bring "this man's blood" upon them (5:28), in spite of the fact that he had been strictly charged no longer to teach in the name.

To a crowd gathered in the temple Peter had once suggested in an impassioned plea for repentance that they had acted in ignorance (3:17). Before the Sanhedrin, however, there is no such leniency extended (4:10, 5:30).

(b) *The resurrection*

The second essential ingredient of the apostolic *kerygma* is the resurrection. In fact, it is the decisive element in the primitive message — the most central of the three great events that formed the historical foundation of the *kerygma*. Had it not been for the resurrection, who would have recognized the redemptive significance of the death? And certainly no one would have dared to assert the exaltation of a dead and buried Jesus. Filson correctly concludes that the resurrection is the rock-bottom fact of Christian life and faith.[45] It is in the light of this central fact that all the other facts receive their significance.

Similar to the death, the resurrection is found in every one of the early speeches (2:24, 32, 3:15, 4:10, 5:30, 10:40). Since the resurrection of Jesus had been prophesied, it was impossible that the bonds of death could have held Him (2:24). David foresaw the resurrection (2:31), which was the fulfillment of God's promise to him that one of his descendants should sit upon his throne (2:30).

One essential item connected with the proclamation of the resurrection was that it had been duly witnessed (2:32, 3:15, 4:20, 5:32, 10:41).[46] Not all saw the risen Jesus; only those

45 Floyd V. Filson, *Jesus Christ the Risen Lord,* p. 31.
46 T. F. Glasson ("The Kerygma: Is Our Version Correct?" *Hibbert Journal,* LI (Jan. 1953), 129-32) is correct in saying that "it is incontestable that this witnessing should be included in any true account of the apostolic preaching" (p. 130).

who had been chosen for this purpose (10:41). It was not a vision, however, because they both ate and drank with Him (10:41).

(c) *The exaltation*

The exaltation of Jesus is the logical sequel to His resurrection. Similar to the death and resurrection, it is woven into the prophetic outlook of the Old Testament (2:34, Ps. 110:1, 3:13, Isa. 53:13, 4:11, Ps. 118:22). This exaltation is to the right hand of God (2:33) as Leader and Savior (5:31). It involves universal Lordship (2:34-35) and the reception of the promised Holy Spirit (2:33). The outpouring of the Spirit is proof of the exaltation of Jesus (2:33). It also is the explanation for the Pentecostal experience of speaking in tongues (2:16-21).

Although the exaltation of Jesus is not explicitly mentioned in the Cornelius speech, it is implied in His ordination as Judge of the living and the dead. Peter would have undoubtedly enlarged upon this aspect of the *kerygma* had he not been interrupted by the supernatural coming of the Holy Spirit (cf. 11:15).

Before leaving the historical section of the *kerygma*, it will be well to explain two apparent omissions. First is the matter of the life and ministry of Jesus. Should some recital of these events be included in a reconstruction of the primitive message? If so, should they assume a major role?

Since Dodd includes the ministry of Jesus along with the death and resurrection as the means whereby the age of fulfillment has dawned, we may assume that he sees it as an essential item in the *kerygma*.[47] Later, in a somewhat lengthy argument, he explains its apparent absence from the Pauline material and concludes that if Paul neglected this aspect, then "in this respect he departed from the common model of apostolic preaching."[48]

What is the evidence of our sources? When we review the early speeches, we are struck by the fact that in only two of

47 Dodd, *The Apostolic Preaching*, pp. 21-22.
48 *Ibid.*, p. 31.

the five is there any reference at all to the life and ministry of Jesus. This fact alone should make us reluctant about elevating it to a place of prominence. But let us examine the two references themselves.

Peter's speech to Cornelius (10:34-43) is generally cited as an example of the *kerygma* in which a historical recital of the life and ministry of Jesus plays an important part. It is explained by the fact that the Gentiles were less acquainted with the basic facts of Jesus' ministry than were the Jews of Judea.[49]

While this is true, it does not account for the appearance of the historical data at this point. Important to note is that Peter is not imparting new knowledge concerning the ministry of Jesus. Rather, he is appealing to a body of facts that they already knew. 'You *know* the word . . . which was proclaimed throughout all Judea," Peter reminds them, and then he sketches the baptism and healing ministry of Jesus (10:36-38). What they did not know was that He had been crucified, and that God had raised Him. Thus, it appears that the "historical section" served primarily to establish the identity of Jesus and was not so much an integral part of the positive proclamation.

The other reference to the ministry of Jesus is found in the Pentecost speech. In Acts 2:22, Peter says that God attested Jesus of Nazareth to them with mighty works, wonders, and signs. Yet here again the statement is conditioned by the preface, "as you yourselves know." Peter is not giving new information concerning the life of Christ, but establishing common ground as a foundation for his following assertions.

This evidence leads us to conclude that the events of the life and ministry of Jesus do not properly enter in a positive way into the initial preaching of the early Church. To say this, however, is not to deny that as time went by and the Gospel began to reach out to a more pagan audience who would know little if anything of the life and ministry of Jesus, a recital of these events would be a necessary introduction to the *kerygma* proper. (Nor is it to suggest that the life of Christ

49 *Ibid.*, p. 28.

is theologically unrelated to His death and resurrection.) It is only to say that as far as we can discern from the evidence at hand, the life and ministry of Jesus play no appreciable role in the initial missionary proclamation. They are overshadowed by the towering significance of the death, resurrection, and exaltation.

A second point in Dodd's reconstruction that needs to be challenged is his inclusion of the second Advent as a major plank in the kerygmatic platform.[50] There are, admittedly, only two verses that can be rallied to support this assertion — Acts 3:20 and 10:42. If the evidence of these verses were direct and unambiguous, we might be inclined to grant the point. But as a matter of fact, the evidence is not.

Acts 10:42 speaks of the apostles' commission to preach that Jesus was the one ordained by God as judge of the living and the dead. Although judgment, in its ultimate sense, requires an eschatological orientation, it cannot of itself be construed to necessitate a second Advent.

The only explicit mention of a return of Jesus is found in Acts 3:20. But notice that even here it bears only an indirect relation to the actual proclamation. It does not take its place among the great and positive facts of redemption, but is brought in later (almost as an afterthought) to strengthen the plea for repentance. This leads us to conclude that the second Advent should not be taken as a primary and essential part of the *kerygma*. When the early preachers were intent upon bringing men to repentance and faith in the risen Jesus, they did not speculate concerning the future, but proclaimed the mighty act of God whereby that redemption had been achieved.

Bound up with Dodd's elevation of this minor item to a place of importance is his view that the early Church looked for the *immediate* return of Christ — "the impending corroboration of a present fact."[51] But whatever their eschatological expectations might have been, one thing is certain: the

50 Dodd, *op. cit.*, p. 23.
51 *Ibid.*, p. 33.

second Advent does not show up as an essential item in their evangelistic message.

On the basis of the paucity of references to the second Advent in the Petrine speeches Glasson asserts that "it is impossible to maintain that the note of imminence is at all prominent, if indeed it is present anywhere."[52] If by this he means that the note of imminence is therefore to be ruled out of the early Church as such, he has taken an unwarranted step. What the apostles believed concerning the return of Jesus, and what they deemed essential in a missionary message designed to bring men to faith, are by no means the same.

2. The resultant evaluation

The exaltation of Jesus leads on naturally to an evaluation of His person. By virtue of the resurrection, Jesus is declared to be "both Lord and Christ" (2:36). The Messiahship of Jesus is the central theological assertion of the kerygma. "All thinking," writes E. F. Scott, "had for its object the proof of the Messianic claim."[53] It is everywhere thrown into bold relief by the repeated proclamation of the resurrection.

In Acts 2:31 and 3:20, Jesus is formally identified as "the Christ." In 3:18, the designation "his Christ" stresses Jesus' personal relationship to God. Once He is called simply, "Christ" (2:36), and in three places the combination "Jesus Christ" is used (2:38, 4:10, 10:36).[54]

In addition to these direct references to Jesus as the Messiah, the early speeches present an astonishing array of titles that reflect the firm grasp of the primitive community on this basic

---

52 Glasson, op. cit., p. 132.

53 E. F. Scott, The First Age of Christianity, p. 183. W. Manson (Jesus the Messiah, p. 2) calls the Messiahship of Jesus the "absolute presupposition of the Church's tradition" — the substratum of all Christian theology. Cf. also Rawlinson, Christ in the Gospels, p. 68, where the confession of Jesus' Messiahship is said to be "a conviction which lies at the very heart of the Christian Gospel."

54 A. Harnack (The Date of Acts and of the Synoptic Gospels, pp. 104-06) argues that in all these verses (except 10:36) χριστός means "the Messiah." The fateful step of treating "Christ" as a proper name was left for a later generation (p. 106).

truth. These names are not Messianic in the sense of technical expressions taken over from the Old Testament but, rather, are established as such by primitive usage.[55] Jesus is called the Holy One (2:27, 3:14), the Righteous One (3:14),[56] the Author of Life (3:15),[57] the Stone (4:11), and the Judge of the Living and the Dead (10:42). We can also hear the Messianic overtones that ring through the titles of Prophet (3:22), Servant (3:13, 26), and Savior (5:31). Although the latter is basically soteriological, its true significance is derived from the broader context of Messianic deliverance.

Along with the primary assertion that Jesus was the Christ was the equally important confession that He was also Lord (2:34, 36, 3:19, 10:36). Contrary to Bousset's assertion that the title "Lord" was a cultic designation current in Hellenism and first applied to Jesus by the Gentile Church, the Lordship of Jesus had its origin in the primitive Aramaic-speaking Church. Its appearance in the early speeches is not anachronistic, but testifies to a primitive evaluation of the risen Jesus. The name itself stresses the moral and religious sovereignty of Jesus the Messiah.

It should be noted that Jesus did not *become* the Messiah by virtue of the resurrection. Rather, it was this event that decisively vindicated Him as such. It was the capstone of His Messianic ministry. At the same time, the resurrection enriched and deepened the very concept it proved. It was to this exalted view of God's Anointed that the early preachers strove to lead their listeners. They argued the death, resurrection, and exaltation of Jesus as the irrefutable proof that He was both the Lord and Christ.

3. *The summons to repent*

The *kerygma* was not a dispassionate recital of historical

---

55 Vincent Taylor, *The Names of Jesus*, p. 73. On pages vii-viii he classifies all the following names (except "Savior") as Messianic.

56 These two concepts, holiness and righteousness, "are drawn from the very fountain of the Messianic idea" (F. H. Chase, *The Credibility of the Book of the Acts of the Apostles*, p. 133).

57 Cf. also Acts 5:31, where ἀρχηγός stands alone.

facts — a sort of nondescript presentation of certain truths, interesting enough, but morally neutral. It was, rather, the existential confrontation of man with the inescapable dilemma of having put to death the very One whom God exalted to universal Lordship. Was there any way by which man could escape the inevitable result of his blasphemous conduct? Only one — Repent! Therefore, the apostolic sermon invariably led up to a call for repentance (2:38, 3:19).[58]

The need for repentance was heightened by the fact that the Jew was a part of a "crooked generation" (2:40) that was living in a state of wickedness (3:26). It was urgent that he repent for there was salvation in no other name (4:12) and disobedience meant sure destruction (3:23).

However, the strongest incentive for repentance was the gracious offer of forgiveness of sins. This was a central feature in the apostolic message. It was explicitly promised in four out of the five speeches (2:38, 3:19, 5:31, 10:43) and implied in the other (4:12). Forgiveness was the blessedness that flowed out to mankind as a result of the humiliation and exaltation of Jesus the Christ. It transformed what would have been merely "news" into what was desperately needed — "good news."

Other results of repentance were "times of refreshing" (3:19) and the reception of the Holy Spirit (2:38, 3:19, 5:32, 10:44). At one point (3:19-20) it is suggested that the return of Christ was contingent upon national repentance.

This, then, according to the speeches in Acts, was the apostolic *kerygma* — a proclamation of the death, resurrection, and exaltation of Jesus that led to an evaluation of His person as both Lord and Christ, confronted man with the necessity of repentance, and promised the forgiveness of sins.

58 Peter's two speeches before the Sanhedrin (4:8ff. and 5:29ff.) are not, in the strictest sense, evangelistic sermons. One is an explanation and the other a defense. While they reflect the content of the *kerygma*, they would include no call to repentance. (However, cf. 4:12 and 5:31.) In the Cornelius speech the tone is milder because the Gentile audience did not share the same guilt as the Jewish nation. Yet, the designation of Christ as Judge (10:42) involves the necessity of repentance.

THE KERYGMA AND THE NEW AGE

It will have been noticed that thus far there has been no mention of the dawning of the Messianic Age. This point is generally felt to be an essential item (if not the ruling concept) in the apostolic message. Dodd gives it pride of place in his *kerygma*[59] and holds that of all the items, the entering of the *eschaton* into history was most "surely primitive."[60] In another place he writes, "Everything else that the Proclamation contains is governed by this maxim: 'The time is fulfilled, and the Kingdom of God is at hand.' "[61] Why then has this apparently essential ingredient been overlooked in the foregoing development?

The primary reason is simply that there is no direct and explicit reference to the coming of the Messianic Age to be found in the early speeches. Nowhere does Peter announce, "The time is fulfilled, the Messianic Age is here." The only verse that could conceivably be so construed is Acts 3:24 with its ambiguous reference to "these days" (the days between the Ascension and the Second Advent?) that have been proclaimed by all the prophets from Samuel on. However, this can hardly pass as a formal proclamation of the inauguration of the Messianic Age.

We must remember that in a historical and literary inquiry of this nature, it is necessary to confine ourselves to the existing evidence. What was actually said must not be confused with what might have been said. Secondly, we must distinguish between the total theological outlook of the early Church and what it would include as relevant in a message designed to bring men to faith.

But what of all the verses that speak of fulfillment? Do they not bear testimony to the arrival of the New Age? That they *imply* this is not denied. But what we must insist upon is that in these references to the fulfillment of prophecy (the suffering [3:18], death [2:23], resurrection [2:31], and exaltation [2:34-35] of Jesus), the immediate point of reference is Christ — not

59 Dodd, *The Apostolic Preaching*, pp. 17, 21.
60 *Ibid.*, p. 34.
61 Dodd, *The Bible Today*, p. 75.

the Messianic Age. In the words of Peter, it is "to *him*" that "all the prophets bear witness" (10:43). In the speeches in Acts, it is Christ who is the subject of prophecy — not the Age He inaugurates. The apostles' preaching centered in concrete historical facts. They proclaimed an event, not an idea.

To say this is not to deny that the Messianic Age did, in fact, come in that cluster of historical events that centered in Jesus of Nazareth. Nor is it to maintain that the apostles did not recognize it as such.[62] It is only to say that the primitive Church in its evangelistic ministry was much more concerned with proclaiming God's mighty act of redemption than in drawing out its dispensational implications.

And is this not true to what we know of Semitic thought? The God of the Jew was One who revealed Himself by laying bare His mighty arm and acting within history. It would have been most unusual if the Jewish-Christian apostles had relegated these stupendous events to a secondary place and couched their message in terms of a somewhat abstract concept.

We conclude, therefore, on the basis of the available evidence, that the Messianic Age, although implied in the *kerygma*, was not a positive element in the actual proclamation. The heart of the apostolic preaching lay in the declaration of God's redemptive act in Christ Jesus. "The Passion story," writes T. W. Manson, "is the core of the primitive preaching in its missionary aspect."[63]

This conclusion is strikingly confirmed by the indirect references in Acts to the preaching of the apostles. Peter's evangelistic address to the crowd in the Temple is summarized by Luke as a "proclaiming in Jesus the resurrection of the dead" (Acts 4:1-2). It was "to the resurrection" that the apostles gave their testimony with great power (Acts 4:33; cf. 11:20). When Philip set out to evangelize the Ethiopian eunuch, he

---

62 Bultmann (*New Testament Theology*, I, 43) goes a step too far when he judges it an exaggeration to say that the earliest Church was directly conscious that the New Age had dawned. It would be better to say that while it recognized that the Last Days had arrived, the full realization of all that this implied was the result of later reflection.

63 T. W. Manson, *The Servant-Messiah*, p. 52.

began with Isaiah 53 and preached to him, not the "New Age," but "the good news of Jesus" (Acts 8:35).

This major emphasis of the primitive message did not change as it reached out to foreign lands. Apollos in Achaia is reported as having "powerfully confuted the Jews in public, showing by the scriptures that the Christ was Jesus" (Acts 18:28). Everywhere we turn in Acts, we find the proclamation of Christ, not the New Age.

The most conclusive evidence of the centrality of the resurrection and Messiahship of Jesus is found in connection with the ministry of Paul. Of the many references to his preaching,[64] we cite but one. At Thessalonica he was "explaining and proving that it was necessary for the Christ to suffer and to rise from the dead, and saying, 'This Jesus, whom I proclaim to you, is the Christ' " (Acts 17:3). Here is no official proclamation of a New Age but a polemic presentation of the crucial facts concerning Jesus of Nazareth.

---

64 Acts 9:20-22, 17:18, 32, 18:5, 23:6, 24:21, 25:19, 26:22-23, and 28:23.

Chapter Six

CLUES TO A PRE-PAULINE KERYGMA

In our effort to reconstruct the primitive *kerygma* we are not limited to the information supplied by the early speeches in Acts. A second and extremely important source is the semi-creedal elements that are found embedded in the Pauline Epistles. This body of material we shall designate as "pre-Pauline." The designation does not mean that the material had necessarily crystallized into a fixed form prior to Paul's conversion. It only indicates that it stems from that "twilight period" between the founding of the Church and the writing of the Pauline corpus. If this material yields a *kerygma* that corresponds in content and emphasis with that of the speeches in Acts, we may then conclude that our reconstruction has been valid and that the resultant *kerygma* faithfully represents what the first apostless actually proclaimed.

But how are we to recognize these pre-Pauline fragments? Is it really possible to distinguish between Paul's own contribution and what he has taken over from his predecessors? While the task is not simple, neither is it hopeless. The primitive strata can be uncovered by the judicious application of certain criteria.[1]

The most obvious indication that a section is pre-Pauline is the apostle's simple statement that he is about to deliver some body of truth that he has received. Fortunately, the most important segment of kerygmatic tradition (I Cor. 15:3ff.) falls into this clear-cut category.

Often it is the style of a passage that betrays its formulary

---

1 Stauffer (*New Testament Theology*, pp. 338-39) lists twelve criteria of creedal formulas in the New Testament. Cullmann (*The Earliest Christian Confessions*, p. 20n.) feels that these are a bit rigid, but accepts the first four and the last as worthy of consideration.

nature. For example, the over-all artistic structure of Philippians 2:6-11, along with its careful paralleling of phrases, is strong evidence that here we are dealing with an early Christian hymn. Further, it has been shown that creedal formulas display a preference for participial and relative clauses. Syntax is usually simple and clear. Often the insertion of a creedal statement results in a break in the context. For the most part, formulary material treats the essentials of the Christian faith, and at times reflects a theological outlook that antedates Paul.

Some may be classified without hesitation as pre-Pauline. Others must be labeled as probable, or perhaps only possible. In the discussion that follows, only those verses that are clearly pre-Pauline will be allowed to exercise a formative influence in the reconstruction.

It should be noted that certain material, although creedal and earlier than the writing in which it is found, will not enter into the present investigation. In this category are the liturgical sequences (such as I Tim. 3:16, II Tim. 2:11-13), simple confessional formulas (Heb. 4:14, I John 2:22, 4:2, 15), and more developed theological statements (II Tim. 2:8) that are found in the later New Testament writings. For example, the confession "Jesus Christ has come in the flesh" (I John 4:2) was certainly in use before John incorporated it; but this does not indicate that its origin dates back to that twilight period with which we are concerned.

Along with this group we must also exclude such bipartite formulas as I Corinthians 8:6. These owe their existence to the struggle against paganism,[2] and are therefore later than the primitive *kerygma*.

There is yet another consideration that enters into the selection of material. Not only must a passage be pre-Pauline, but it must also be kerygmatic. Since we have taken Dodd's definition of preaching ("the public proclamation of Christianity

---

2 Cullmann, *op. cit.*, p. 46. I Cor. 8:6 is designated by Cullmann as the "prototype of confessions with more than one article" (*loc. cit.*). Cf. also I Tim. 2:5-6, 6:13ff., and II Tim. 4:1.

to the non-Christian world") as determinative,[3] it follows that
the *kerygma* is distinctly soteriological. It is a message that,
above all else, is designed to bring men to faith. This limits
our primary inquiry to those pre-Pauline passages that bear
direct testimony, not to the general life and faith of the early
Church, but to her missionary message. Verses like Ephesians
5:14 — although an excellent example of a pre-Pauline baptismal hymn[4] — will not enter into our investigation, because
they shed no light on the nature of apostolic preaching.[5]

Concerning each passage, therefore, two questions will be
asked: (1) Is it genuinely pre-Pauline?, and (2) Is it kerygmatic? With those two criteria in mind, let us proceed.

I CORINTHIANS 15:3ff.

This passage is without doubt the most valuable piece of
pre-Pauline Christianity in the New Testament. Not only is it
authentic tradition, but it also furnishes direct evidence of the
missionary *kerygma* proclaimed by the early Church. It relates
the very terms[6] in which Paul (v. 1) and the others (v. 11)
preached the Gospel.

What are the reasons for accepting this account of the Gospel
as genuine pre-Pauline *paradosis*?

(1) The verbs that Paul uses for the reception and trans-
mission of the Gospel are equivalent to the official Jewish
terms for the taking over and passing on of tradition.[7] This

3 Cf. above, p. 65.

4 A. M. Hunter (*Paul and His Predecessors*, p. 45) suggests that this
baptismal hymn of exhortation was sung by the onlooking congregation
at the moment when the convert would rise from the baptismal wave.

5 After careful consideration, I Thess. 1:9b-10 is being omitted from
the present investigation. Dibelius (*Thessalonicher* I/II (HNT), p. 5, and
the excursus on the rhetorical style of 1:2 — 2:16, pp. 10-11) argues that
this is a concise statement taken over from the terminology of the apostolic mission, and deliberately employed in order to strike a responsive
chord in their memories. This may be so, but the verse still tells what
they did, not what they heard. The indirectness of the evidence places
these verses outside the category that we are to study.

6 τίνι λόγῳ ("in what terms") refers to both the form and the substance of Paul's preaching.

7 Dibelius, *From Tradition to Gospel*, p. 21. *Pirke Aboth* 1:1 tells how
Moses *received* the (oral) Law from Sinai, and *committed* it to Joshua.

would indicate that what follows is to be understood as an authentic block of primitive material.

(2) The total structure of the passage with its fourfold repetition of ὅτι ("that") indicates that it is a creedal formulation.

(3) This formula displays a number of un-Pauline characteristics: (a) The phrase "according to the scriptures" occurs nowhere else in Paul[8] (who generally uses "as it is written"). (b) Since for Paul ἁμαρτία (singular) is the principle of sin, it is doubtful that he would have used it in the plural, as in verse 3. (c) Certain other expressions, such as "the twelve," are not specifically Pauline.[9]

(4) The double reference to the Old Testament Scriptures suggests that it stems from a Jewish-Christian source. So also does the Aramaic "Cephas," and the reference to James.

(5) Paul indicates in verse 11 that what he has reproduced has been the common proclamation of all the apostles.

It is not going beyond the evidence to conclude with Meyer that here we have the oldest document of the Christian Church in existence.[10]

But now we come to the more difficult task of defining the limits of this segment of *paradosis*. Had Paul stopped quoting as decisively as he began, there would have been no problem. But he seems to add a parenthetic remark, extend the final issue, and then trail off into a personal testimony. In view of this we must ask, Where does the *kerygma* stop, and Paul begin?

The explanatory remark connected to the phrase "more than five hundred brethren," leads Goguel to strike out all of verse six as a Pauline addition.[11] The following phrase ("Then he appeared to James, then to all the apostles") is taken as genuine *kerygma* because of its linguistic similarity to verse 5.

---

8 Interestingly enough, the only other occurrence of this phrase is in James 2:8 — most certainly Palestinian in origin.

9 For further linguistic evidence, see Jeremias, *The Eucharistic Words of Jesus*, pp. 129-130.

10 H. A. W. Meyer, *Ursprung und Anfänge des Christentums*, III, 210.

11 Maurice Goguel, *The Birth of Christianity*, p. 42.

The appearance to Paul, says Goguel, was added as a personal testimony.

While something can be said for this interpretation, it is much more probable that the original formula extended from 3b through verse 5. This gives a better balance to the entire passage and brings the final item into harmony with the conciseness with which the other three are set forth. This division is also supported by the definite syntactical break at the beginning of verse 6. The reason for expanding this particular section of the *kerygma* was to establish firmly the fact of Christ's resurrection. From this basic premise, Paul will argue the resurrection of the believer. The choice of witnesses — well-known leaders of the Church and a large body of people who could easily be found and questioned — shows the care with which Paul built his case.

Where and when did Paul receive this block of tradition? The usual answer is that it was passed on to him by Peter when they first met in Jerusalem for a fortnight visit (Gal. 1:18-20) i.e., about A.D. 35.[12] This does not, however, take into sufficient consideration Paul's prior ministry in Damascus (Acts 9). Paul's proof of the Messiahship of Jesus (v. 22) most certainly rested upon the kerygmatic foundation of Christ's death, resurrection, and exaltation.

It is much more likely that this bit of *paradosis* had a much earlier origin. Hunter suggests that Paul is here reproducing the baptismal creed of the Damascus church.[13] A comparison with the baptismal formula that underlies I Peter 3:18-22 favors this view.[14] But whatever its relationship to baptismal or catechetical confessions, it is primarily the terms in which the Gospel was *preached* (cf. v. 1). It is difficult not to infer from this that it was originally drawn up as a convenient summary of the missionary proclamation.

And where did it originate? Against Heitmüller's thesis that it was an evangelical summary current in Hellenistic Chris-

12 Dodd, *The Apostolic Preaching*, p. 16.
13 Hunter, *op. cit.*, p. 16. Cf. also J. N. D. Kelly, *Early Christian Creeds*, p. 17.
14 Note the similar pattern: death for sins, descent, resurrection, exaltation.

tianity and radically different from the Palestinian *kerygma,*
Hunter argues convincingly that it emanated originally from
the primitive Palestinian church.[15] If this be so, then I
Corinthians 15:3-5 may represent the very message that won the
first converts at Damascus. In any event, we may safely conclude that Paul received this kerygmatic summary from the
Damascus church shortly after his conversion and before beginning his evangelistic ministry.

Let us now set this passage out as it might have looked had
Paul used sermon notes:

> Christ died for our sins —
>   in accordance with the scriptures.
> He was buried.
> He was raised on the third day —
>   in accordance with the scriptures.
> He appeared to Cephas,
>   then to the Twelve.

But is this all there was to the primitive *kerygma?* Where
is the conclusion that this One is therefore "both Lord and
Christ?" And where is the call to repentance?

What we have here is obviously just a fragment of the total
kerygma. Paul is not giving a comprehensive report of how
he went about bringing men to faith in Christ. He is reminding the Corinthians that the resurrection was a fundamental
part of the message that they had accepted. While this segment
of *paradosis* gives a crystal-clear picture of the historical section
of the *kerygma,* it does not tell the complete story. In order to
see the total message in its proper perspective, we must look
elsewhere.

ROMANS 10:9

An excellent example of this proper balance is Romans
10:9 — "If you confess with your lips, 'Jesus is Lord,' and believe in your heart that God raised him from the dead, you
will be saved."

That this kerygmatic summary is pre-Pauline, there is little
doubt. The very way in which it is introduced leads us to

15 Hunter, *op. cit.,* pp. 16-17.

expect something from the common Christian faith. It is a concise summary of the "word of faith" that was everywhere proclaimed by the apostles and the missionary Church.[16] Since Paul assumes his readers' knowledge of this "word of faith," we may infer that it is both common to all the apostles and pre-Pauline in origin.

Linguistic evidence supports this conclusion. Throughout the New Testament, God is repeatedly described as the One who "raised him [Jesus] from the dead" (Rom. 4:25, 8:11, II Cor. 4:14, Gal. 1:1, Eph. 1:20, Col. 2:12, I. Pet. 1:21). The creedal quality of this phrase is seen even more clearly in the Greek, by its particular choice of both verb and preposition. Add to this the fact that the phrase "Jesus is Lord" is the earliest single-clause Christological confession of primitive Christianity, and one will agree that here we have "an old creedal formula which bears all the marks of a genuine creed and should be viewed as a preparatory step to the later Christian confessions of faith."[17]

Now let us examine the passage more closely. It maintains that salvation is contingent upon a twofold confession. Man must first believe that Jesus was raised from the dead. Then he must confess Him as Lord. These are the two fundamental pillars of the apostolic preaching — resurrection and Lordship. Towering above all the more incidental elements, they majestically proclaim the message of redemption.

And is this not exactly what we found in the early speeches of Acts? First, there was a setting forth of the death, resurrection, and exaltation of Jesus. In our present summary, these three inseparable events are characterized by the one that is most central and decisive — the resurrection. Then we found that this led on to an evaluation of the person of Jesus as "both Lord and Christ." In Romans 10 the confession "Jesus

---

16 If verse 9 be taken in direct apposition to "the word of faith," then ὅτι will be translated "namely." It is also possible that ὅτι is recitative and introduces the answer to the question asked by the righteousness based on faith (v. 8). Either way, however, the ὅτι clause gives the content of the primitive message. Cf. Bultmann, *Theology of the New Testament*, I, 89.

17 H. Sasse, "Jesus Christ, the Lord," *Mysterium Christi*, p. 93.

is Lord" answers perfectly to this. This harmony of content and emphasis leads us to conclude in a tentative way that there are no broad discrepancies between the *kerygma* in Acts and what we have found in the main pre-Pauline passages.

ROMANS 1:3-4

There are other fragments of pre-Pauline *paradosis* that strengthen this conclusion. Although they do not purport to give direct evidence of the actual "word of faith," they do reflect the theological atmosphere of the early Church. They should therefore be brought into the discussion as confirmatory evidence.

The most important of these secondary testimonies is the Christological confession in Romans 1:3-4. Even when read in English, this passage has a creedal ring. Similar to other Christological formulas, it was constructed by attaching to the name of Jesus certain incidents in the redemptive story.[18] It enters the present context as an appositional modifier of "concerning his Son" (v. 3). As is customary with so many creedal formulations, its structure is developed along the lines of an underlying contrast — in this instance, "according to the flesh". . . "according to the spirit." This is accomplished by using two carefully paralleled participial clauses.[19]

Having granted that the passage is a creedal formulation, we must now ask if it is genuinely pre-Pauline. Could it not owe its symmetrical form to Paul's creative ability?

Several considerations make this unlikely. In the first place, Paul is trying to establish common ground with a group of Christians to whom he has never ministered. To accomplish this, and to accredit himself as a preacher of sound doctrine, he cites a common confession of faith that would be known and recognized at Rome. If Paul had been sketching his own doctrine of the person of Christ, it most certainly would have surpassed this primitive and somewhat inadequate formulation.

18 Kelly, *op. cit.*, p. 18.
19 τοῦ γενομένου..., τοῦ ὁρισθέντος... Cf. D. P. Fuller and R. H. Mounce, *Sentence Diagrams of Romans, ad loc.*, for structural analysis of this creedal formulation.

There are other and more concrete indications of its pre-Pauline origin. The reference to Jesus as the seed of David is not Pauline.[20] It is found here because it was already present in the primitive confession that Paul incorporated into his opening words to the Romans.

Professor Hunter cites the "adoptionist Christology" as another un-Pauline element in the passage.[21] The adoptionist interpretation generally rests upon the argument that "spirit of holiness" is a Hebraistic expression for the Holy Spirit whose descent "appointed" Jesus "Son of God" and equipped Him with Messianic power.[22]

There is no doubt that the verse will lend itself to such an interpretation. There is good reason, however, to believe that adoptionism was not in the author's mind when he penned this bit. In the first place, it is extremely doubtful whether "spirit of holiness" is to be understood as a Hebraistic equivalent of "Holy Spirit." This would break down the anti-thetical parallelism that lies at the base of the entire formulation. The contrast between flesh and spirit requires that they be predicated of the same person.[23] It is more probable that "spirit of holiness" refers to Christ's human spirit, but distinguished from the merely human spirit by an exceptional and transcendent holiness.[24]

20 The Davidic descent of the Messiah was a prevailing concept in the early Church (Mark 12:35ff., Ps. Sol. 17:27ff., IV Ezra 12:32) and Christians pointed to Jesus' lineage as having fulfilled one of the conditions of Messiahship (Acts 2:20, Heb. 7:14).

21 Hunter, *op. cit.*, p. 28. Paul's Christology is incarnationist. Cf. Rom. 8:3, Gal. 4:4.

22 Johannes Weiss (*The History of Primitive Christianity*, I, 119; also II, 476) finds in this passage both a primitive adoptionism ("appointed Son of God") and a Pauline alteration ("with power"). This collision of two modes of thought is said to account for the harsh construction of verse 4.

23 Sanday and Headlam, *Romans (International Critical Commentary)*, p. 9.

24 In the first ten chapters of Acts, the Holy Spirit is designated Πνεῦμα Ἅγιον a total of twenty-five times. If this be the terminology of the primitive Palestinian church, we would most certainly have expected it in the pre-Pauline creed — that is, if the writer had been actually speaking of the Third Person of the Godhead.

In the second place, it is unlikely that "in power" was meant to be linked with "Son of God." It is much more natural to take it adverbially with "designated" to mean "mightily declared."

Finally, while it is true that the uncompounded ὁρίζω in Acts 10:42 and 17:31 is best rendered "appointed," this meaning can hardly be applied to its occurrence in 11:29 ("The disciples *determined* . . . to send relief"). The exact shade of meaning must in each instance be determined by the context. Therefore, in Romans 1:4 we are not under compulsion to understand the participle as a semi-technical term for "appointment" or "installation."

Rawlinson, in an appended note ("On the alleged 'Adoptionism' of Primitive Christianity"), charges those who find evidence of early adoptionism in the New Testament with the failure to distinguish between the Jewish-Christian and the Gentile-Christian conceptions of what was meant by divine Sonship.[25] For the Jew it involved no more than a recognition of function. It expressed no theory of ultimate nature. Since the Gentile church received their theology of Sonship from Jewish-Christian apostles, there was no opportunity in the opening decades of Christianity to explain Christ's Sonship in terms of the pagan concept of apotheosis.

Furthermore, if Paul was concerned with accrediting himself to Rome as an apostle of sound doctrine, is it likely that he would have put his stamp of approval upon a Christological concept that he knew to be false? While the passage is clearly pre-Pauline, it cannot be argued from any "adoptionist Christology."

What, then, does it teach? It teaches that Jesus, in reference to His human lineage, descended from David, but that, in reference to His spiritual heritage, He was by the resurrection mightily declared to be the Son of God. He is therefore Jesus Christ, our Lord. Even if one should prefer the triadic division of the Peshitta[26] (which on other grounds is im-

25 A. E. J. Rawlinson, *The New Testament Doctrine of the Christ*, pp. 265-69.

26 Cf. Hunter (*op. cit.*, pp. 26-28) for a translation of the Syriac and a favorable treatment of this conjecture.

probable), the above interpretation would not be impossible. That Jesus was anointed with "power and holy spirit" at baptism would not rule out the possibility of a further mighty declaration of His Sonship by means of the resurrection.

With these technical questions aside, we may now inquire what light this passage throws upon the *kerygma*. Like the more direct evidence of Romans 10:9, it emphasizes the very same kerygmatic items that the speeches in Acts emphasize. Once again the resurrection is given a central and decisive role in the drama of redemption. It is this mighty act of God, more than any other, that proclaims to all men everywhere the divine Sonship of Jesus. That Jesus is the Messiah is indicated both by the reference to His Davidic descent and by the title "Son of God." The idea of Messiahship has not been entirely subdued in the name "Jesus [the] Christ." And, finally, just as the Lordship of Christ was the goal of all the sermons in Acts, so is it in this primitive creed.

Thus, while the creed is not *kerygma* (in the strictest sense of the word), it is by all means kerygmatic. It brings into focus the very same items that we found to be the basic assertions of all apostolic preaching.

ROMANS 4:24-25

There are two other passages in Romans that bear witness to the content of the pre-Pauline *kerygma*. The first is Romans 4:24-25, where the "creed-like note is unmistakable."[27] Let us review the reasons for this confident assertion.

(1) The introductory "those who believe" leads us to expect some sort of summary of early Christian belief.

(2) The stereotyped phrase "who raised him from the dead" has been shown to be a pre-Pauline article of faith.[28]

---

27 Kelly, *op. cit.*, p. 20. Cf. also Lietzmann, *Romans* (HNT) pp. 24-25, and Bultmann, *op. cit.*, I, 82. Bultmann also includes Rom. 3:24ff. among those passages where Paul is "visibly leaning on traditional formulations" (*ibid.*, p. 46). We have, however, by-passed this "possible source" because to arrive at it Bultmann must first excise a large number of Pauline expressions and because such a method is haunted by arbitrariness.

28 Cf. above, p. 94.

(3) The combination of participial and relative clauses, clearly seen in the Greek text, is an indication of formulary style.

(4) The synthetic parallelism of members is also strong evidence that we are dealing with a creedal statement.

It may be objected, however, that the concept of death for sins and the idea of justification are not primitive, but reflective and late. That the early Church saw from the very first a vicarious significance in the death of Christ is proved by I Corinthians 15:3 ("Christ died for [ὑπέρ] our sins") and by I Corinthians 11:24 ("This is my body which is broken *for you*"). The appeal to the Scriptures (especially Isa. 53) and the references in Acts to Jesus as the Servant of God show that from the very first the death of Christ was interpreted in the light of the Suffering Servant of Isaiah. In our present passage, the deliberate choice of the verb παρεδόθη ("was delivered over"; cf. Isa. 53:12, LXX) is a conscious attempt to effect this interpretation. It is not anachronistic to maintain that Jesus' being delivered up "for our trespasses" was part of a pre-Pauline confession.

But what of the reference to justification? While the fully developed doctrine of justification by faith is a characteristic Pauline doctrine, its roots reach far into the past. Did not Paul, in Galatians 2:15ff., maintain that even those who were Jews by birth knew that a man is not justified by works of the law? There is no ground for holding that the term "justification" could not have occurred in a primitive confession. Weiss is right in reckoning Romans 4:25 "among the doctrinal statements which St. Paul derived from the early church."[29]

ROMANS 8:34

Before summarizing the content of this passage, let us go on to a similar fragment of pre-Pauline *paradosis*, which is found embedded in Paul's inspiring words concerning the love of God (Rom. 8:34). This closely knit creedal statement may be arranged as follows:

29 Weiss, *op. cit.*, I, 104.

> Christ Jesus,
>   the one who died,
>   (or rather, who was raised),
>   who is at the right hand of God,
>   who even intercedes on our behalf.

The rhythmical movement of the verse, the careful paralleling of clauses,[30] the marked preference for participial and relative clauses, and the antithetic and anaphoral style, all testify to the fact that here we have a primitive and creedal statement of faith. Since the thought of intercession was "deeply fixed in early Christian belief," we here stand entirely on the ground of the original preaching of the Gospel.[31]

COMPARING SOURCES

Let us now compare these two segments of pre-Pauline Christianity with the two that give direct evidence of the primitive *kerygma* (I Cor. 15:3-5 and Rom. 10:9). To show, at the same time, their correspondence with the *kerygma* of Acts, they may be organized according to the following outline:

A. Death
    "Christ died for our sins" (I Cor. 15:3).
    "Jesus . . . who was put to death for our trespasses[32] (Rom. 4:24-25).
    "It is Christ Jesus who died" (Rom. 8:34).

B. Resurrection
    "He was raised on the third day" (I Cor. 15:4).
    "Raised for our justification" — "Him that raised from the dead Jesus" (Rom. 4:25, 24).
    "Who was raised from the dead" (Rom. 8:34).

C. Exaltation to Lordship
    "If you confess with your lips, 'Jesus is Lord'" (Rom. 10:9).

---

30 Chester Beatty, Vaticanus, Bezae, the Koine, and the majority of the Old Latin translations, all add καί after the first ὅς. This reflects an attempt to create an even more symmetrical structure.

31 Dodd, *Romans*, p. 144.

32 Since the διά of the parallel clause is definitely prospective ("to bring about justification"), it should be understood in the same way here (that is, "in order to atone for our trespasses"). Cf. Gifford, *Romans*, pp. 108-09.

"Jesus our Lord" (Rom. 4:24).
"Who is at the right hand of God" (Rom. 8:34).[33]
Two conclusions may be drawn from this comparison. First, that the creedal statements of Romans 4:24b-25 and 8:34 reflect almost perfectly the essential items of the pre-Pauline *kerygma*. Apart from the single reference to intercession (Rom. 8:34) they may be subsumed in their entirety under the existing kerygmatic outline. Since they do not purport to be *kerygma* proper, this is striking confirmation of the centrality given to the death, resurrection, and exaltation to Lordship of Jesus in the primitive faith.

The second conclusion is that the comparison buttresses our original contention that there exist no broad discrepancies between the *kerygma* of Acts and that of the pre-Pauline tradition.

THE KERYGMA AS PRE-THEOLOGICAL STATEMENT

We turn now to deal more specifically with a problem that has already been raised — that is, Did the early Church actually see in the death of Christ a vicarious significance? Was the phrase "for our sins" (I Cor. 15:3) an interpretive addition to an otherwise pre-theological formula, or was it a genuine part of the original *kerygma*? To help answer this problem, let us investigate a most important segment of pre-Pauline *paradosis* — the words that instituted the Lord's Supper and that Paul had delivered to the church at Corinth (I Cor. 11:23ff.).

It will be immediately noticed that the style of the passage is elevated and liturgical.[34] The opening phrase ("the Lord Jesus") conveys the feeling of ceremonial proclamation. Παρεδίδοτο (usually translated "he was betrayed") is more than a simple chronological statement. It refers to an action of God. The detailed description of the rite has contemporary analogies

33 Dodd (*The Apostolic Preaching*, p. 15) notes that all verses that speak of Christ being at the right hand of God have for an ultimate reference Ps. 110:1. Thus, the phrase "at the right hand of God" is but another way of expressing the Lordship of Christ.
34 Most of the following linguistic points come from Jeremias, *The Eucharistic Words of Jesus*, pp. 107-08, 112, 131.

in ritual texts and should be regarded as a liturgical rubric.
The article in front of "cup" points to the ritual "cup of
blessing" (cf. I Cor. 10:16). All these facts show that we are
here dealing with a highly liturgical formula.

The passage has a number of un-Pauline characteristics.
Several of the words occur only here in Paul.[35] The neat
μετὰ τὸ δειπνῆσαι ("after supper") cannot be paralleled elsewhere in the Pauline writings. When Paul speaks of "the
body" of Christ, he means the Church and not the body of the
man Jesus.

Thus, we conclude with Otto that I Corinthians 11:23ff. is
"clearly traditional material long since rounded off."[36] It is
the eucharistic liturgy of some pre-Pauline church.[37]

But does not Paul expressly say that he received it from the
Lord? Is he not referring to the substance of a special divine
revelation?[38] Although a cursory reading of the text might
suggest that this is so, there are a number of indications that
human channels were the immediate agents through which the
tradition came to him:

(1) Paul uses the same technical terms for "receiving" and
"delivering" as he does a few chapters later (15:3-5). By all
the canons of interpretation they should be understood in the
same sense.

(2) Paul's use of ἀπό instead of παρά in the phrase, "from
the Lord," shows that he is referring to the ultimate source
rather than the immediate agent.[39]

(3) When this segment of eucharistic liturgy is compared
with the Synoptic accounts, there are too many points of similarity not to posit some common source.

If Paul received it from some primitive congregation, where
and when could this have taken place? Damascus is always a
possibility. Outside the city he was converted. Three days

---

35 δειπνέω, ὁσάκις, and ἀνάμνησις (twice).
36 Rudolf Otto, *The Kingdom of God and the Son of Man*, p. 326.
37 Hunter, *op. cit.*, p. 21.
38 So H. Lietzmann, *Messe und Herrenmahl*, p. 255.
39 By way of comparison, see Acts 20:24, where he speaks of receiving
his ministry *from* (παρά) the Lord. This choice of preposition corresponds
to the directness of the commission.

later he regained his sight and was baptized by Ananias. It was undoubtedly in Damascus that Paul was initiated into the sacramental table fellowship of the Christian community. Thus it seems probable that Damascus was that crucial point in his spiritual history where he received the Words of Institution as well.

Jeremias, however, detects a certain linguistic remolding of the *paradosis* which would require the lapse of a greater period of time.[40] For example, the great majority of Semitisms in Mark's account are either avoided or graecised.[41] This is the type of thing that would take place in a Hellenistic environment for the sake of the Greek reader and would normally require more than the some four years between the crucifixion and Paul's conversion. Jeremias therefore suggests that Paul has taken over the formula in use at Antioch where he settled about A.D. 40.[42] In either case, however, the tradition enshrined within the narrative originally stems from the Jerusalem church and ultimately from those present in the Upper Room.

With these prolegomena aside, we can now investigate what light this pre-Pauline liturgical formula throws on the early Church's understanding of the death of Christ. Was it a death "for sins"? Was there at least this much theological "superstructure" in the primitive *kerygma?*

Consider the following evidence:

(1) The phrase "on the night when he was *delivered up*" refers to the action of God.[43] It echoes Isaiah 53 (note v. 12 especially) and involves as a background for interpretation the total concept of the Suffering Servant.

40 Jeremias, *op. cit.,* pp. 127, 131.

41 εὐλογήσας becomes εὐχαριστήσας, πολλῶν is replaced by ὑμῶν, etc.

42 R. H. Fuller (*The Mission and Achievement of Jesus,* pp. 65-68) argues against the Antiochian origin. His most suggestive contribution is that since Paul used Damascus as a headquarters for missionary work in Arabia, and since the Damascus church had undoubtedly received and was celebrating the Eucharist, it is almost incredible to suppose that Paul waited some seven years until he had moved to Antioch before he began introducing the Eucharist in the churches.

43 The passive, as in Rom. 4:25, is a "reverential passive" and denotes that God is the subject of the action.

(3) The action of Jesus in breaking the bread indicated that as the loaf was then broken, so also was His body to be broken in the near future. The distribution of the broken loaf indicated that the disciples were to share in the atoning power of His death.

(3) When Jesus said, "This is my body," He intended to be understood as referring to the sacrificial offering of Himself in death.[44]

(4) Jeremias gives detailed evidence to show that behind the Greek σῶμα ("body") lies the Aramaic bisrā.[45] The twin concept, bisrā udhemā, signifies the component parts of a sacrificial victim which are separated when it is killed. Thus, Jesus' crucial terms are chosen from the vocabulary of sacrifice.

(5) The phrase "which is for you [ὑπὲρ ὑμῶν]" more than any other one item emphasizes the vicarious nature of Christ's death. The ὑμῶν is a liturgical alteration of Mark's πολλῶ' (the communicants would wish to feel themselves personally addressed by the Lord). The latter is to be interpreted in terms of Isaiah 53, with the common Semitic inclusive meaning of "the sum total, consisting of the many" — that is, the whole world. Thus, Christ interprets His death as a vicarious sacrifice that atones for the sins of the whole world.

Additional evidence could be brought to bear, but sufficient has been cited to show that the pre-Pauline liturgical formula of I Corinthians 11 definitely teaches that Christ died "for our sins." Thus there is no reason to refuse the testimony of the kerygma as it stands in I Corinthians 15: that in accordance with the Scriptures, "Christ died for our sins." This insight into the significance of Christ's death was not a later theological development, but part of the very warp and woof of the primitive proclamation.

From the two segments of pre-Pauline paradosis that purported to give the actual content of the apostolic preaching (I Cor. 15:3-5 and Rom. 10:9), we arrived at a kerygma that was identical in both content and emphasis with that of the

44 V. Taylor, Jesus and His Sacrifice, p. 121.
45 Jeremias, op. cit., pp. 140ff.

early speeches in Acts. Then we investigated three primitive creedal formulas in Romans (1:3-4, 4:24b-25, 8:34) and found that, although not *kerygma* in the strictest sense of the word, they supported the previous conclusion in a striking manner. Following this, we turned aside to investigate the eucharistic tradition of I Corinthians 11:23-25. This segment of early Christian liturgy substantiated the kerygmatic claim that Christ's death was "for our sins."

THE LORDSHIP OF CHRIST IN THE PRE-PAULINE MATERIALS

One item remains — to emphasize the centrality of the Lordship of Christ in the apostolic ministry. This may be done by noting the creedlike expressions of Lordship that are scattered throughout the Epistles. In II Corinthians 4:5, Paul epitomizes the ministry of the first evangelists by saying, "For what we preach is not ourselves, but Jesus Christ as Lord." Again, in I Corinthians 12:3, he refers without explanation to the earliest confession of the Christian Church — "Jesus is Lord." Throughout the Pauline corpus one hears these terse formula-like phrases recurring like a never ending refrain ("All those who call upon the name of our Lord Jesus Christ," I Cor. 1:2; "One Lord, Jesus Christ," I Cor. 8:6; "As you received Christ Jesus the Lord," Col. 2:6; etc.). The Aramaic liturgical invocation that is transliterated in I Corinthians 16:22 as μαρ&να θᾶ ("Our Lord! Come!")[46] is unassailable proof that the confession of Christ's Lordship is to be traced back to the primitive Palestinian church.[47]

In addition to these incidental references, there is one particular segment of pre-Pauline Christianity that highlights in a most important way the Lordship of Christ. It is the Christ-hymn of Philippians 2:6-11. There are abundant indications that this hymn is an authentic piece of pre-Pauline liturgy. Its artistic structure, rhythmic style, and stately bearing, all

46 The use of μαρανάθα in *Didache* x. 6 establishes it as eucharistic invocation. (Chapters 9-11 treat the general subject.) Note also the entreaty, "Come, Lord Jesus!" in Rev. 22:20.

47 Cf. Foerster, in *Theologisches Wörterbuch zum Neuen Testament, sub* κύριος ; Gregory Dix, *Jew and Greek,* p. 79.

betray a ceremonial character. It stands out in almost vivid contrast to the narrative style of the surrounding verses. Its terse phrases[48] are characteristic of liturgical formulas.

That it did not first flow from the pen of St. Paul is seen in both vocabulary and diction. It contains distinctive words that are found nowhere else in Paul. In fact, two of them[49] do not occur anywhere else in the entire New Testament.

A good deal of evidence has been brought forward by Lohmeyer to show that the author's mother tongue was Aramaic, not Greek.[50] Closely connected is the fact that, while Paul customarily used the LXX, this hymn reflects the Hebrew Bible. For example, the difficult ἑαυτὸν ἐκένωσεν can only be understood as a translation of the Hebrew הֶעֱרָה ... ‎. This united testimony is conclusive evidence that the hymn was firmly entrenched in the liturgy of the Church before it ever came into the hands of Paul.[51]

Where did Paul receive it? Any answer to this question comes dangerously close to pure speculation. Lietzmann[52] and Lohmeyer[53] hazard the guess that it was part of the eucharistic liturgy of some Palestinian church. Not finding the distinctive overtones of the Palestinian church, Hunter surmises that Paul found it in the churches of Syria (perhaps Antioch).[54] Whatever its origin, it is decidedly primitive, and therefore valuable evidence for our conclusions about the *kerygma*.

As to the original structure of the hymn, there have been

---

48 e.g., τὸ εἶναι ἴσα θεῷ.

49 ἁρπαγμός, ὑπερυψοῦν.

50 Ernst Lohmeyer, *Kyrios Jesus*, pp. 8ff.

51 Stauffer (*New Testament Theology*, p. 284, n. 372, p. 246) says that this hymn must be Pauline because it is an incarnation, not a passion, formula. This argument is without force because the participial clauses that refer to Christ's human life are only inserted in a parenthetic way to bridge the gap between the pre-existent state of glory and the humiliation of the Cross. The "Kenosis" here taught is properly that of the *Crucifixion*, not the *Incarnation*. Cf. H. Wheeler Robinson, *The Cross in the Old Testament*, pp. 104-05.

52 Lietzmann, *Zeitschrift für die neutestamentliche Wissenschaft*, XII (1923), 265.

53 Lohmeyer, *op. cit.*, pp. 65ff.

54 Hunter, *op. cit.*, p. 49.

a number of suggestions. Widely accepted has been the reconstruction of Lohmeyer.[55] Starting with the observation that διὸ καί in verse 9 divides the hymn into two equal parts, he arranges it in six strophes of three lines each. The subdivisions are made on the basis of the particles ἀλλὰ...καί, and ἵνα...καί. The first three verses speak of the humiliation of Christ; the second three of His exaltation.

A different (and more probable, I believe) division is suggested by Jeremias.[56] He rejects the six-verse arrangement on the basis that four of the six strophes trail off without a proper ending. He maintains that the hymn is built up by *parallelismus membrorum* and has three strophes of four lines each.[57] Besides the last phrase of verse 8 ("even death on a cross"), which Lohmeyer had already designated as a Pauline addition, Jeremias takes "in heaven and on earth and under the earth" (v. 10) and "to the glory of God the Father" (v. 11) as not part of the original hymn.[58] This threefold division is said to furnish the oldest example of the doctrine of the three *Seinsweisen Christi* — the pre-existent, the earthly, and the exalted.

We come now to the interpretation of the hymn and its relationship to the *kerygma*. While agreeing with Jeremias that Christ's three "modes of existence" are reflected in its structural pattern, we must be careful not to assume that this is its central significance. When the author speaks of Christ not

55 Lohmeyer, *op. cit.*, pp. 5-6.

56 Jeremias, "Zur Gedankenführung in den paulinischen Briefen," *Studia Paulina*, pp. 152-54.

57 A division into three strophes is also maintained by L. Cerfaux (*Le Christ dans la théologie de saint Paul*, pp. 283-98), but the arrangement is slightly different (1st strophe as far as "form of a servant" in v. 7, 2d through v. 8, and vv. 9-11 forming the 3d). Cerfaux argues a Pauline authorship for the hymn, and marshals linguistic evidence to show that the Servant Songs of Isaiah were the apostle's principal source. Cf. E. Käsemann, "Kritische Analyse von Phil. 2:5-11," *Zeitschrift für Theologie und Kirche*, 47 Jahr. 3 Heft) for a summary of still other treatments.

58 The first phrase is separated from its noun by the verb, and both "heaven" and "earth" are favorite Pauline words. The adverbial phrase belongs to the verb "shall confess" and is thoroughly Pauline.

grasping after equality with God, he is not laying down a formal doctrine of pre-existence, but giving the background of the Servant's humiliation. An appropriate title for the hymn (as determined by its own progression of thought) could be, "Voluntary humiliation resulting in exaltation."

Using as clues the concepts of the two Adams and the Suffering Servant, A. M. Hunter gives the theme of the hymn as "Jesus, the Second Adam who, conquering the temptation to which the First Adam fell, chose the role of the Suffering Servant and for his obedience unto death was highly exalted by God, and made 'Lord' of the whole cosmos."[59]

We may now relate the hymn to the apostolic preaching in two ways. First, if the foregoing interpretation be correct (and there is every reason for accepting it), it supports our conclusion that the primitive congregation understood the death of Christ in terms of the Suffering Servant, and therefore, as a vicarious and expiatory sacrifice.[60]

Secondly — and this is even more important to our present inquiry — it presents as the crowning significance of the Servant's redemptive "Kenosis," the exaltation and Lordship of Jesus Christ. Here, embedded in an ancient liturgical hymn, is evidence that the climactic confession "Jesus Christ is Lord" was the governing concept of primitive Christian thought. Not only was this confession the goal towards which all apostolic preaching moved, but it represents the very atmosphere of the life and worship of the first Christian congregations. No matter how far we move back into the dawn of apostolic preaching, there we find as its very heart and core the proclamation that Jesus of Nazareth is "both Lord and Christ." This is the testimony of all the evidence — whether it be taken from Peter's early sermons in Acts, or from the fragments of primitive tradition embedded in the Pauline Epistles.

We conclude with the words of Cullmann who, in his search for the "essential content of the Gospel," comes to the conclu-

59 Hunter, *op. cit.*, pp. 46, 49-51.
60 H. Wheeler Robinson, *op. cit.*, p. 113.

sion that "it is . . . the present Lordship of Christ, inaugurated by His resurrection and exaltation to the right hand of God, that is the centre of the faith of primitive Christianity."[61]

61 Cullmann, *The Earliest Christian Confessions*, p. 58.

Chapter Seven

QUESTIONING THE ORIGINS OF THE PRIMITIVE PROCLAMATION

IN the course of the last two chapters we have worked our way through the available source material and have determined as accurately as possible the message that was proclaimed by the first heralds of Christianity. Starting with the speeches in Acts (which we argued to be authentic summaries of what was actually said), we found that the *kerygma* consisted in a historical proclamation, a theological evaluation, and an ethical summons. The pre-Pauline material, on examination, was found to substantiate the tentative reconstruction in a most convincing manner. We therefore concluded that both sources testified to a common apostolic *kerygma*.

In the present chapter we intend to ask several important questions about the origins of this apostolic proclamation. In the first place:

ARE THERE ANY REAL DISCREPANCIES BETWEEN THE SOURCES?

We have contended that, in both content and emphasis, the two sources of the *kerygma* have been in general agreement. But what of those residual points of difference? Do they have reasonable explanations, or should they cause us to speak less confidently about *the* apostolic message? Let us examine three apparent discrepancies.

While the *kerygma* of Acts describes Jesus in titles taken from Isaiah, it never once designates Him "Son of God" — as in Romans 1:3-4, for example. Does this mean that we have wrongly tried to integrate two distinct levels of apostolic tradition? That this "omission" forms a discrepancy that is apparent rather than real is made clear by the following observations:

(1) The idea that Jesus, as Messiah, is the Son of God is

deeply rooted in the Synoptic tradition.[1] On the basis of the Q saying, Luke 10:22 and Matthew 11:27[2], and the undeniably authentic Mark 13:32 (as well as the Baptism and Temptation stories, plus the Parable of the Wicked Husbandmen), it may be shown that the title "Son of God" is grounded in the thought and teaching of Jesus Himself.[3] The reason that He never directly designated Himself as such is that Sonship for Jesus meant "not a dignity to be claimed, but a responsibility to be fulfilled."[4] The title stems from an early tradition that reflected the mind of the historical Jesus, and therefore it cannot be used as evidence of a more developed stage of the *kerygma*.

(2) The evidence of Mark 12:35-37 and 14:61 ("Are you the Christ, the Son of the Blessed?") shows that in the time of Christ Psalm 2:7 was, in some circles at least, interpreted Messianically.[5] Thus, the title "Son of God" would convey the same general meaning as the Acts designation, "Lord and Christ" (Acts 2:36). Any minor deviation in terminology between the sources is without real significance.

(3) It would also be most unreasonable to expect a complete correspondence in every minor point. Since the titles of Sonship were associated more with the teaching ministry of the primitive communities than with their evangelistic preaching,[6] it would be perfectly natural to find Jesus referred

1 Jesus is so designated by the Voice from Heaven (Mark 1:11, 9:7), Satan (Matt. 4:3, 6), demons (Mark 3:11, 5:7), the High Priest (Mark 14:61), and the centurion (Mark 15:39).

2 While the genuineness of this "Johannine thunderbolt" has been quite regularly denied by Continental scholars (M. Dibelius, *From Tradition to Gospel*, pp. 279-83; Bousset, *Kyrios Christos*, pp. 45-50; Johannes Weiss, *The History of Primitive Christianity*, I, 120-21, n. 73), the arguments against its authenticity are not conclusive. For a more favorable view see W. Manson, *Jesus the Messiah*, pp. 71-73; V. Taylor, *The Names of Jesus*, pp. 64-65; T. W. Manson, *The Teachings of Jesus*, pp. 109-10.

3 V. Taylor (*Jesus and His Sacrifice*, p. 35) judges that Mark 13:32 (one of Schmiedel's nine "foundation-pillars for a truly scientific life of Jesus") is conclusive proof that Jesus spoke of Himself as "the Son."

4 R. H. Fuller, *The Mission and Achievement of Jesus*, p. 84.

5 C. G. Montefiore, *The Synoptic Gospels*, I, 351.

6 The two writers who show a decided preference for the Sonship terminology are the author of Hebrews and the writer of I and II John.

to as "Son of God" in a confessional formula like Romans 1:3-5, but not so likely in a direct account of the missionary preaching.

(4) If "Son of God" were the product of an advanced Christology, Paul's frequent and natural use of it (e.g., Gal. 2:20) would be most surprising.

Therefore we conclude that the absence of the title "Son of God" from the speeches in Acts constitutes at the most only an apparent discrepancy between the sources.

A second deviation between the *kerygmas* is the statement in Romans 8:34 that the exalted Christ intercedes for us. Because of the remarkable symmetry of this primitive creed, it is very unlikely that this one member of its antithetical structure would be a Pauline insertion.

While there is no direct reference to intercession in the speeches in Acts, there is considerable mention of exaltation to the right hand of God (2:25, 33, 34, 5:31) and the forgiveness of sins (2:38, 3:19, 5:31, 10:43). Does this not express the idea of intercession in terms of its occasion and resultant blessings? Entirely apart from these considerations, however, we should bear in mind that Romans 8:34 does not purport to give direct evidence of the preached message. This alone is sufficient explanation for the "omission" of intercession in the *kerygma* in Acts.

A third difference between the two *kerygmas* is that in the speeches in Acts there is no direct assertion that Christ died "for our sins." In the former chapter we argued at length that this theological evaluation of Christ's death was an integral part of the earliest preaching. Why then is it apparently missing in the speeches in Acts?[7]

To begin at the circumference of the problem, we should

---

7 This problem is well stated by J. Weiss (*The History of Primitive Christianity*, I, 113-16), although his explanation (that Luke possessed sources older than Mark which did not see Christ's death as a propitiatory sacrifice, and that he preferred to use these older forms) is not acceptable. A more recent writer who claims that the *kerygma* in Acts attaches but little value to the death of Jesus is J. R. Branton (*Religion in Life*, XXVI [Winter, 1956-1957], p. 12).

first remind ourselves that the doctrine of death for sins cannot be Pauline in origin, for he explicitly states that it was part of the *paradosis* that he had "received" (I Cor. 15:3-5). Flew suggests that since Luke is here writing a second volume, he cannot be expected to repeat what he has already stated in the first.[8] He also suggests that evangelical preachers do not always establish this relationship before bringing their hearers to repentance and faith in Jesus Christ as Lord. While the first suggestion makes the speeches more Lukan than Petrine, and the second is a bit suspect, both admit that death for sins is absent from the *kerygma* in Acts.

A more adequate answer is that while mention of death for sins does not occur in Acts as a stereotyped formula, it is the constant background of thought. The very fact that Peter twice in one sermon refers to Jesus as the "servant" (παῖς) of God (Acts 3:13, 26) opens the way to interpret Christ's death along the lines of Isaiah 53.[9] Let us expand this suggestion.

Of the five New Testament references to Jesus as the Servant of God, all but one (Matt. 12:18) are found in the first chapters of Acts (3:13, 26, 4:27, 30). The substantive is ambiguous and may mean "child" as well as "servant," but it is quite certain that as applied to Jesus the latter meaning is the one intended.[10] This is confirmed by the observation that in Gentile Christianity, where the term would not be able to rid itself of the objectionable connotation of servitude, there are virtually no references to Jesus as the Servant of God.[11] This remarkable avoidance of the term in reference to Jesus is only explainable on the basis that it meant "servant" rather than "child."

But is it not possible that Servant of God is simply a title of

8 R. Newton Flew, *Jesus and His Church*, p. 123.

9 C. H. Dodd, *The Apostolic Preaching*, p. 25

10 A. E. J. Rawlinson (*The New Testament Doctrine of the Christ*, p. 241) would posit an original Aramaic tradition behind these passages in which the Messiah was described unambiguously as the "Servant" of the Lord.

11 In all the Gentile Christian literature up to A.D. 160, παῖς θεοῦ is found only eleven times, and in all but one instance it is connected with the liturgy of prayer. Cf. Zimmerli and Jeremias, *The Servant of God*, pp. 83-84.

honor, and not a direct reference to the Suffering Servant of Isaiah? This is unlikely in view of the many direct and indirect allusions to Isaiah 53 that occur throughout the speeches in Acts. By way of example, let us examine Peter's speech in Acts 3.

Acts 3	Isaiah 53[12]	
v. 13 "God . . . glorified his servant whom you delivered up"	52:13	"my servant . . . shall be glorified"[13]
	53:6	"the Lord delivered him up"
v. 14 "the righteous one"	53:11	"the righteous one"[14]
v. 18 "that his Christ should suffer"	53	the entire chapter portrays the sufferings of the Servant

This comparison makes it clear that it was in terms of the Suffering Servant of Isaiah 53 that Peter proclaimed the death of Jesus. This is not surprising, however, when we remember the extensive role played by this chapter in the life and thought of the early Church. C. H. Dodd has gathered evidence to show that virtually every verse in the Suffering Servant poem of Isaiah 52:13-53:12 is represented in one way or another in almost every part of the New Testament.[15] The influence of Isaiah 53 is seen in the pre-Pauline kerygmatic summary of I Corinthians 15:3-5, in various primitive Christological confessions (Rom. 4:25, 8:34), and in the liturgy of the Eucharist (I Cor. 11:23-25) and the worshipping Church (Phil. 2:6-11). The ease with which the whole series of free quotations from Isaiah 53 is applied to Jesus in I Peter 2:21-

12 The comparison is best seen in the Greek text.

13 This identification is strengthened by the fact that Acts 3:13 is the only text in the Synoptics or Acts in which $\delta o\xi \acute{a}\zeta \epsilon \iota \nu$ has the meaning "to transfigure."

14 It is possible that the Messianic title "The Righteous One" finds its origin in this verse. Cf. V. Taylor, *The Names of Jesus*, p. 82.

15 *According to the Scriptures*, pp. 92-94.

25 is evidence of a widely accepted identification.[16] Jeremias concludes his survey of the Christological interpretation of the Isaianic Servant with the statement, "There is no area of the primitive Christian life of faith which was not stamped and moulded by the *'ebed* christology."[17]

We conclude that while in the speeches in Acts there is no stereotyped statement that Christ died "for our sins," they everywhere interpret His death in terms of the Suffering Servant whose role was to bear the sins of the many. There is no basis for contending that discrepancies exist between speeches in Acts and the pre-Pauline *kerygma*. The two sources unite to proclaim one common apostolic message.

There can be little doubt that this common apostolic *kerygma* represents a very early stage in the proclamation of the Gospel. We have seen that Paul received it at a date not later than seven years after the crucifixion. It does not follow from this, however, that the *kerygma* must be primitive in the strictest sense. It is within the bounds of possibility that there could have been considerable development in those first tumultuous years of the new Faith. We will do well to consider carefully this problem.

IS THE KERYGMA REALLY PRIMITIVE?

Incompatible Christologies?

J. A. T. Robinson has argued that in the early speeches of Acts we are met with "two *incompatible Christologies.*"[18] The speech in Acts 2, with its creedlike summary ("God has made him both Lord and Christ") , is taken as a polished specimen of what later became the established norm of apostolic preaching. In Acts 3, however, we are moving in a different atmosphere. Here, like a fossil of a bygone age, lies the "first tentative and embryonic Christology of the early

16 This passage, along with others such as Acts 8:27-39, is taken by C. R. North (*The Suffering Servant in Deutero-Isaiah*, p. 26) as decisive proof "that the early Church did interpret the cross in the light of Isa. liii."

17 Jeremias, *The Servant of God*, p. 98.

18 J. A. T. Robinson, "The Most Primitive Christology of All?" *Journal of Theological Studies*, VII, New Series (Oct. 1956) , 177-89.

Church." At this point, Jesus is not yet seen as Messiah. He
is rather the Messiah-elect whose mission on earth has been
to act as His own forerunner. Robinson builds his case by
arguing that the titles "Lord" and "Christ" in Acts 2 are late
and represent a stage in that process (which had its logical
beginnings in Acts 3) whereby the Church pushed its Christology back into the life of Jesus.

Robinson admits that the shift from seeing Jesus as the
Messiah-elect to the realizing that in the Cross-and-Resurrec-
tion the eschatological event had actually taken place, and
that consequently from then on Jesus was the Messiah, may
have taken place by the day of Pentecost.[19] If this were true,
then his thesis would not be relevant to our immediate problem; because whatever might have been the psychological development of the pre-Pentecost days, it would have little
bearing on the theological growth of the post-Pentecost *kerygma*. The entire tenor of the article, however, is to confirm the
priority of Acts 3 and suggest that Acts 2 represents a later
position.

If this could be proved, we would have to admit that our
kerygma would represent an advanced stage in apostolic
preaching and could not be considered as truly primitive. That
we are not forced to such an alternative is quite clear for the
following reasons:

(1) Certain evidence has to be overlooked in denying that
the terms "Lord" and "Christ" are typical of the most primitive *kerygma*. In addition to the three references to Jesus as
Christ that meet us in the Pentecost speech (2:31, 36, 38), His
Messiahship is also maintained in 3:18 (which will be shown
not to be a Lukan addition), 3:20, 4:10, and 10:36. If Leader
and Savior (5:31) are accepted as Messianic titles,[20] then we
are faced with the fact that in every single early speech in Acts,
Jesus was preached as the Christ. That He was also Lord is
the abiding significance of the exaltation — mention of which
occurs in every early speech.[21]

<hr />

19 *Ibid.*, p. 185.
20 Cf. above, p. 83.
21 Note also the "ejaculatory parenthesis" in 10:36 ("He is Lord of
all").

(2) Robinson realizes that the statement in Acts 3:18 that Jesus suffered as the Christ is absolutely fatal to the hypothesis that he is being presented as the Messiah-elect. His attempt to get rid of it as a Lukan interpolation is far from convincing. How can it be maintained that the idea of a suffering Jesus "plays no part in any other formulation of the primitive κήρυγμα,"[22] when the other speeches refer to His death in terms of crucifixion "by the hands of lawless men" (2:34), "rejection" (4:11), and killing "by hanging him on a tree" (5:30, 10:39)? If this is not suffering, what is it?

(3) The idea that Jesus came as His own forerunner is built on a foundation that is hermeneutically unstable. Not only is the immediate passage admittedly difficult, but the interpretation that is thrust upon it can nowhere else find confirmation. And what does this do to John the Baptist? Whose forerunner does he become? Furthermore, the hypothesis asks us to believe that the primitive Church simultaneously held two completely diverse concepts of the mission of Jesus. He would have to be both His own "Elijah" who had come to turn Israel to repentance (3:20), and at the same time the Servant of God (3:13, 26) who came to bear the sins of the many.

The theory has other weaknesses, but enough have been disclosed so that we need not be unduly concerned about an alleged dual Christology in the earliest tradition.

Historical Scepticism

The primitiveness of the *kerygma* is also impugned by those who approach the Scriptural data with an air of historical scepticism. H. J. Cadbury maintains that in addition to historical theology, there is also a theological history, namely, a proclamation of events based on theology.[23] As forces at work in the pre-*kerygma* development, he lists (among others) logical inference, the creative influence of the Old Testament, and the practical necessity of furnishing a doctrinal basis for

---

22 Robinson, *op. cit.*, p. 183.

23 H. J. Cadbury, "Acts and Eschatology," *The Background of the New Testament and Its Eschatology*, p. 300.

certain ethical exhortations. He feels that Dodd's formulation of the *kerygma* is defective in that, overlooking these creative forces, it ignores the unequal age and origin of its several parts. "Catch the apostolic preaching as early as you can," asserts Cadbury, "but you must still admit that development preceded as well as followed that date."[24]

Varying degrees of liberty have been taken with this general approach. A conservative scholar like H. E. W. Turner will admit a certain element of discrepancy between the details in the resurrection narratives; yet he insists that the empty tomb and the appearances are two authentic strands of evidence.[25] Weiss, on the other hand, says that the empty grave is "the creation of unfettered fancy," and the "massive resurrection stories must first have originated upon Hellenistic soil, for the purposes of missionary apologetics."[26]

Even more sceptical is Goguel, who would have us believe that the resurrection, at bottom, was but the restoration of the disciples' confidence in Jesus afer a momentary eclipse caused by the crucifixion.[27] What was at first a mystical and psychological experience eventually took on the aspect of an affirmation of fact and was ultimately turned into a doctrine.[28]

What can be said about historical scepticism and its relationship to the *kerygma?*

In the first place, in its milder forms it affects only the peripheral issues of the *kerygma*. The central affirmation of the resurrection does not stand or fall on the authenticity of such items as "the third day," or one's ability to harmonize the "Galilean" and "Jerusalem" traditions.

If scepticism extends to the actual resurrection itself, then we need only to pause long enough to request an explanation for the "most gigantic and successful swindle in human history."[29] Turner aptly says, "Men who have the lie in the soul do not behave as the disciples do in the rest of the New

24 *Ibid.,* p. 319.
25 H. E. W. Turner, *Jesus, Master and Lord,* p. 361.
26 Weiss, *op. cit.,* I, 91, 87.
27 M. Goguel, *The Birth of Christianity,* p. 74.
28 *Ibid.,* p. 86.
29 T. W. Manson, *The Servant-Messiah,* p. 91.

Testament: a changed life based upon a conscious fraud is a moral impossibility."[30]

The possibility of development is much more real, however, when we come to the sphere of interpretation. Even if we acknowledge the death and resurrection of Jesus as the historical foundation of apostolic preaching, could it not be that the interpretative element in the *kerygma* was the fruit of subsequent reflection?[31]

We might be forced to yield to this line of reasoning — and so relinquish any hope of maintaining that the *kerygma* was truly primitive — but for the very real possibility that the interpretation of the crucial events actually had its roots in the life and teaching of Jesus Himself, and was not simply the product of the Church's religious insight.[32] If this be so, there would be no necessity of positing a long period of time during which the primitive congregation would ponder the implications of Calvary and Easter, and finally arrive at their theological significance. If it can be shown that Jesus had already indicated the meaning of His Passion and supplied the necessary raw materials for a Christology, there would be no reason to doubt that the mighty act of the resurrection (supplemented by the interpretative ministry of the risen Christ[33]) was the catalyst that, prior to the earliest preaching, crystallized the interpretative element involved in the *kerygma*.

This does not mean that the Church would have begun its ministry with a full-fledged theology. Not even today has the theology of the Cross reached a state of static completeness.

30 Turner, *op. cit.*, p. 370. See also James Denney, *Jesus and the Gospel*, pp. 108-59.

31 Bultmann ("New Testament and Mythology," *Kerygma and Myth*, pp. 1-44) holds that the *kerygma* is an attempt of the early Church to interpret the earthly history of Jesus as a redemptive event by the use of mythological terminology.

32 This is the major thrust of Fuller's helpful book, *The Mission and Achievement of Jesus*.

33 Insufficient attention has been given to verses like Luke 24:45-46 and Acts 1:3 in this connection. Canon Hunt, however, (*Primitive Gospel Sources*, pp. 39-50) holds that the first Testimony Book was born of the teaching received by the disciples between the resurrection and the ascension.

It would only be to say that from the first the *kerygma* was fact plus interpretation, and that this interpretation was not "prophecy after the event" but the result of a natural development that had its origins in the teachings of Jesus. Let us investigate this crucial question.

DO THE INTERPRETATIVE ELEMENTS IN THE KERYGMA STEM FROM THE TEACHING OF JESUS?

The two most far-reaching interpretative elements in the *kerygma* are the redemptive significance of the death of Jesus and the evaluation of His person as Lord and Christ. Let us examine these separately to determine whether or not they are arbitrarily imposed ideas.

There are three possible ways to account for the interpretation of the death of Christ that meets us in the *kerygma*. The first possibility is that Jesus was silent about His coming death and it fell to His disciples to think up some theological significance for it.

To accept this view is to admit that Jesus was either too naïve to see the increasing hostility, or that He was unable to give an explanation for it. In either explanation His role as leader has been fatally undermined. Furthermore, we must assume that the some twenty independent sayings that the Evangelists ascribe to Jesus concerning His death are the creation of the Church.[34] That a group of "not many wise . . . not many noble" should possess such creative ability is simply too great a strain on the imagination. The more creative the community, the more we are haunted by the question, Who or what created the community?

A second possibility is that Jesus did speak of His death, but that the disciples turned a deaf ear and went on their own way when it came to interpreting the event. The Gospels tell a story that leads irresistibly to a dramatic climax at Calvary. The rest of the New Testament reflects the same emphasis and presents the death of Christ as the burning focus

---

34 Bultmann (who would fall within this category) asks incredulously concerning the Passion predictions, "Can there be any doubt that they are all *vaticinia ex eventu?*" (*Theology of the New Testament*, I, 29).

of God's redemptive activity for man.   Is this the creation of a headstrong Church?

Hardly so, for this would mean that the earliest Christians evidently felt that they knew better than Jesus Himself the meaning of what He was doing.   Not only does this undermine the Church's exalted view of the risen Christ, but it places us under the obligation to accept anything they might decide to dogmatize.   Furthermore, this view raises the unanswerable question as to where the disciples received their clue for interpretation.   It could not have been from the Jew, for to him the Cross was an insurmountable offense to his preconceptions of divine omnipotence and glory.   Nor could it have been from the Gentile, who considered it a blank negation of the Greek idea of a reasonable principle at the heart of things.[35]   Clearly, the significance attached to the death of Christ in the *kerygma* could not have come from the general ideas of redemption.   And not the least objection to this entire approach is that it throws us into complete scepticism as to what Jesus might originally have intended.

It appears, then, that we are shut up to the third possibility, namely, that Jesus did speak of His approaching death, and that the explanation He offered was not disregarded, but became the source for all subsequent development.   This is certainly the most reasonable explanation.   It protects the originality of Jesus, defends the integrity of the disciples, and answers best to the Scriptural data which we possess.

Let us then turn to the Passion Sayings to see how Jesus interpreted His approaching death.

Jesus interprets His death

As early as Mark 2:20, Jesus hints of His coming death.[36] His reference to the Bridegroom being taken away indicates that early in His ministry He had faced the enigma of a dying Messiah.   At a later date He answers the Pharisees' warning about the malicious intent of Herod by implying that death

35 W. Manson, *Jesus the Messiah*, p. 161.
36 Although this saying belongs to a section of Mark that is arranged topically, it undoubtedly is correctly placed before Caesarea-Philippi.

in Jerusalem is to be the appointed culmination of His entire ministry (Luke 13:32). Divine necessity had laid hold of Him (Luke 17:25).

In the Markan narrative there are three formal prophecies of the Passion — 8:31, 9:31, and 10:33-34. In each instance the disciples fail to grasp the significance of the prediction, so it is repeated in such a way as to include them in its broader application. There is no sufficient reason for labeling these fundamental texts as "prophecies after the event."[37] They present Jesus as foreseeing His death and resurrection, and moving towards that goal with dogged determination.

But what significance did Jesus attach to His coming death? Was it to be no more than a martyr's fate? Hardly so. In the Parable of the Vineyard (Mark 12:1-11) Jesus quietly assumes that He fulfills a role greater than the prophets. He is God's unique Son who is acting as final envoy to Israel. Their violence to Him will result in divine judgment and rejectio..

In speaking of His death Jesus employs three significant metaphors. In the first place it is a baptism that He must undergo (Luke 12:50, Mark 10:38).[38] Since water is used as a symbol of calamity (Ps. 42:7, Isa. 43:2), Jesus is here referring metaphorically to His being plunged into the raging waters of the Passion.

Jesus also speaks of His Passion as a cup that He is to drink (Mark 10:38, 14:36). It is noteworthy that of the twenty Old Testament references where the word "cup" is used metaphorically, seventeen stand for divinely appointed suffering. In drinking it to the dregs, the "cup of woe" (Isa. 51:17-23) is to become the "cup of salvation" (Ps. 116:13).

As a final metaphor, Jesus speaks of His Passion as a road to be traveled. "The Son of man goes as it is written of him" (Mark 14:21). It was also written of the Son of man that "he should suffer many things and be treated with contempt" (Mark 9:12b). What other road could this be but the

37 For a satisfactory treatment of the authenticity of these verses (and all the other Passion Sayings that will enter into this discussion), see V. Taylor, *Jesus and His Sacrifice.*

38 These three metaphors are suggested by A. M. Hunter in his book *The Work and Words of Jesus,* pp. 96-97.

via dolorosa of the Suffering Servant. Although it is only in Luke 22:37 that Jesus explicitly claims to fulfill the role of the one portrayed in Isaiah 53, it would be sheer scepticism to hold that this chapter is not the interpretative background for the great majority of the Passion Sayings.[39] It follows from this that Jesus, in line with the mission appointed for the Suffering Servant, must have interpreted His approaching sufferings as representative and vicarious.

This leads us to the all-important Passion prediction of Jesus in Mark 10:45: "For the Son of man also came not to be served but to serve, and to give his life as a ransom for many." Here again we see the formative influence of Isaiah 53. It is "to serve" that the Son of man has come. This service was the giving of Himself as a "ransom for many." The idea of substitution is present both in the noun[40] and in the preposition (literally, "instead of"). As in Isaiah 53:11, 12a, and 12c, this service is for the "many." Thus, we are justified in interpreting the self-dedication implied in the ransom-word in the light of the Servant's ministry of redemptive suffering. This is most certainly the seed-plot for the ultimate proclamation that "he died for our sins."

This conclusion is buttressed by the teaching of Jesus in connection with the Last Supper. Suffice it to say that every chief word used in the eucharistic formula is saturated with sacrificial significance. In establishing the Sacrament, Jesus portrayed His approaching death as a sacrifice of atoning efficacy and likened Himself to the Passover lamb.[41] The redemptive significance of His Passion was undoubtedly the burden of Jesus' *Haggada* on that last fateful night.

39 Fuller (*op. cit.*, pp. 55-57) joins together the portions of the five Markan prophecies that cannot be the result of subsequent reflection, and finds that they form a clear description of the Suffering Servant. Three of the phrases are summaries of the Servant's fate ("to minister," "to suffer," and "to be killed") and all the others — with one exception (which exception I am not prepared to grant, for παραδίδωμι need not be taken in a non-theological sense) — appear to be direct reproductions of the language of the Hebrew text of Isa. 53.

40 λύτρον is a perfectly adequate rendering of the Hebrew *'asham*, trespass-offering (Isa. 53:10).

41 A. J. B. Higgins, *The Lord's Supper in the New Testament*, p. 51.

It would be impossible to adduce more convincing proof
that the redemptive significance that we find attached to the
death of Jesus in the *kerygma* was in no wise an arbitrary interpretation that the disciples imposed upon an otherwise non-
theological fact of history. There is every reason to believe
that the earliest Christians simply took up and applied the
meaning that Jesus had already taught concerning His death.
Filson writes, "The only satisfactory explanation of the universal apostolic emphasis on the cross is that the life and
message of Jesus himself had already prepared them to think
and preach as they did."[42] We are thus led to the conclusion
that the interpretation involved in the phrase "Christ died for
our sins" is part and parcel of the most primitive *kerygma*.

The raw materials for a Christology

The other main element of interpretation in the *kerygma*
is the declaration that Jesus is the Messiah. This Christological
confession is the theological assumption that underlies the
entire corpus of New Testament writings. "No stratum of
tradition capable of being isolated by the methods of literary
analysis reveals a non-Messianic basis."[43] This means that even
before the tradition as we have it had begun to crystallize,
Jesus was already acknowledged as the Messiah of Israel. Here
we are standing at the very dawn of Christian history.

Our immediate problem is to determine whether this confession represents the unaided religious insight of the disciples, or whether it is grounded in the intention of Jesus
Himself.

The first alternative has been championed by Bousset. It
forms the starting point of his much cited book, *Kyrios
Christos*. Bousset believed that it was the Church who first
transferred the royal mantle of the transcendent Son of man
to the crucified Jesus. When Jesus died, so also did His disciples' hopes that He would prove to be the national Messiah.
But the indestructible impression of Jesus' personality lived
on, and before long they crowned Him as the apocalyptic Son

42 Floyd V. Filson, *Jesus Christ the Risen Lord*, p. 114.
43 W. Manson, *op. cit.*, p. 3.

of man who through suffering and death had entered into glory.

This theory — and all other theories that explain the Church's Messianic confession as a halo placed around the head of Jesus by enthusiastic Jewish religionists — is met with the insuperable difficulty of the ignominy of Jesus' death. For the Jew, the cross carried the inevitable stigma of divine excommunication (Deut. 21:23, Gal. 3:13). Only on the basis that Jesus had already unfolded His role as Messiah and Son of man would it have been possible for Jewish worshippers to ascribe Messianic power and dignity to the one who had borne the curse of sin.

This consideration by itself furnishes strong incentive to accept Manson's premise that "somewhere, somehow, Jesus before his death stood self-revealed to his disciples as the Messiah."[44] But let us also survey the textual evidence.

The designation of Jesus as "Christ" occurs in the caption of Mark (1:1) and quite frequently in the birth narratives of the other Synoptics.[45] Jesus refers to the "Christ" in His discussion of David's Lord (Mark 12:35) and again in His warning about false claimants in the last days (Mark 13:21).[46] In Luke 4:41 is the Evangelist's explanation that the demons were not allowed to speak because they knew Jesus to be the Christ.

Of more interest are the places where the title was referred more directly to Jesus. At Caesarea Philippi, when Jesus asked His disciples concerning their views of His identity, Peter answered, "You are the Christ" (Mark 8:29 and parallels). At the foot of the cross the mocking ecclesiastics derisively addressed Him as "Christ, the King of Israel" (Mark 15:32). The false witnesses before Pilate testified that Jesus had claimed to be Christ, and that His Messianic ambitions had perverted

44 *Ibid.,* p. 11

45 Twice in Luke and five times in Matthew.

46 The phrase 'because you bear the name of Christ' in Mark 9:41 is probably a textual corruption. The use of the term 'the Christ' in Matt. 23:10 is somewhat similar and has the appearance of an explanatory comment.

the nation (Luke 23:2). On none of these occasions, however, did Jesus make a direct reply. It was only at the very close of His ministry, when placed under oath by the High Priest, that Jesus laid clear claim to the title. To the question, "Are you the Christ, the Son of the Blessed?" Jesus answered a frank, "I am" (Mark 14:61-62).

This evidence indicates that while Jesus did not reject the title, neither did He employ it as a self-designation. What accounts for this remarkable reserve?

One clue may be found in the manner in which He accepted Peter's confession. He did not compliment Peter on having arrived at the ultimate significance of His person and mission, but rather He began at once to redefine the concept that lay at the heart of the confession in terms of suffering. The simple truth is that although He was the Messiah, He was not the Messiah that they had expected.

This is not to suggest that there was a uniform picture of the Coming One. He had been portrayed in many ways — as a second and greater David, a warrior Messiah (Ps. of So. 17:23-51), and a supernatural and transcendent Savior. Nor is it to suggest that the disciples' Messianic hope was no more than the bloody subjugation of all nations. It is only to say that since Messianism (even at best) was inevitably linked with national supremacy,[47] Jesus could have no part in it. "My kingship," He said, "is not of this world" (John 18:36). It is this Messianic cross-purpose between Jesus and His contemporaries that explains His reluctance to assume the title. To have overtly claimed to be the Messiah would have been to blur the true significance of His redemptive mission, as well as to have courted a premature reckoning with Rome.

To penetrate more deeply into Jesus' understanding of His mission, we shall have to look elsewhere. It is unnecessary at this point to become involved in a long discussion of the origin

---

47 T. W. Manson ("The life of Jesus: some tendencies in present-day research," *The Background of the New Testament and Its Eschatology*, p. 218) suggests that "to recapture the visions that floated before the mind's eye of a first-century Jew in Palestine when words like 'Messiah' and 'Kingdom of God' were used, we shall probably be well advised to think in something very like Zionist terms."

and significance of the various Messianic titles. A few observations concerning the general lines of development will be sufficient.

It was the title "Son of man" that became the distinctive self-designation of Jesus. This somewhat vague concept with its apocalyptic background (Dan. 7:13ff.) was adopted by Jesus and fused with the role of the Servant in such a way as to interpret His Messianic destiny both in terms of the supernatural being of apocalyptic tradition and of the Suffering Servant of prophecy. The fact that the apostolic age made no use of the title "Son of man" is sure evidence that its use in the Gospels goes back to Jesus.

What led Jesus to make this startling combination of sovereignty and sacrificial service? Does it not ultimately stem from His unique filial consciousness? Sonship, for Jesus, was patterned after that of Israel who, having been chosen by God, was to have responded in filial love and obedience. Obedience for Jesus involved the path of humility marked out for the Suffering Servant. Only through death could the Son of man enter into His exaltation.

Although Jesus did not come to teach a doctrine of His person, it was unavoidable that, in fulfilling His destiny as the Bringer of Messianic salvation, He should also have furnished His disciples with what R. H. Fuller has called "the raw materials of Christology."[48] His entire life and mission were Messianic. Apart from this basis, they are completely unintelligible.

How, then, can it be supposed that the designation of Jesus as Messiah was the arbitrary imposition of a group of determined-to-worship disciples? To the contrary, the origins of this Christological confession lie deep within the intention of Jesus Himself. To hold that it was due to the unaided speculation of the early Church is to fly in the face of all probability. The only reasonable explanation of all the facts involved is that Jesus had gradually unfolded to His disciples His destiny as the one through whom God was bringing Mes-

48 Fuller, *op. cit.*, pp. 79-117.

sianic deliverance, and that the apostolic confession of His
Messiahship was the natural expression of this conviction.

The movement of this chapter has been to show that from
the very first there was but one *kerygma,* and that this *kerygma*
was in every sense primitive. We agree most heartily with
Fuller's final conclusion that "the Church's *kerygma* is not an
abitrary interpretation imposed upon an arbitrarily selected
stretch of history, but that it has an intelligible basis in that
history, and in the mind of the chief participator in it."[49]

49 Fuller, *op. cit.,* p. 117.

Chapter Eight

IMPLICATIONS OF THE CHRIST-EVENT

Now that we have traced the origins of the *kerygma* back into the teaching of Jesus, let us reverse our direction and follow its subsequent development as reflected in the writings of the various New Testament authors.

In *The Apostolic Preaching,* Dodd maintains that the principal cause for the development of early Christian thought was the unexpected delay in the Lord's return.[1] The early Christians are pictured as breathlessly awaiting the *immediate* advent of Christ. God's mighty act of redemption had passed through its crucial stages and "now trembled upon the verge of its conclusion."

Christ did not, however, return. The tremendous crisis in which the early Christians felt themselves to be living passed without reaching its expected issue. This perplexing turn of events thrust upon them the necessity of readjusting their eschatological outlook.

Some minds which were primarily oriented towards the future reacted by taking the apocalyptic materials at hand and reconstructing a modified Jewish eschatology in such a way as to explain the delay. But this line of development led into a blind alley. "In the second century its stream of thought ran out into the barren sands of millenarianism, which in the end was disavowed by the Church."[2]

On the other hand, the delay gave to finer minds the occasion of "grasping more firmly the substantive truths of the Gospel, and finding for them a more adequate expression."[3] This "authentic line of development" is best seen in Paul's

---

1 Dodd, *The Apostolic Preaching,* pp. 31-37 especially.
2 *Ibid.,* p. 41.
3 *Ibid.*

129

transformation of eschatology into "Christ-mysticism" and John's restatement of the entire Christian Gospel in terms of "realized eschatology."

While we are much indebted to Professor Dodd for many of his keen insights, there is reason to question his reconstruction at several vital points.

In the first place, it is not certain that the primitive Church expected the *immediate* return of Christ. They undoubtedly visualized the consummation as taking place within their lifetime, but this is not an "any-moment" expectation.[4] The following points should be borne in mind:

(1) In the early chapters of Acts there is but one reference to the return of Christ (Acts 3:20). This is not what we would expect if the early Church was possessed with forebodings of the end. Furthermore, in this single reference there is no indication whatsoever that the coming is to take place immediately. On the contrary, Christ must remain where He is until the time when God will establish all that He has foretold through the prophets. If the early Church daily expected Christ's return, Luke certainly displays an uncanny ability in avoiding any telltale reference to this primitive "obsession."

(2) There is good evidence that Jesus foresaw an interval and instructed His disciples concerning it. Even if the Apocalyptic Discourse of Mark 13 be reduced to a bare minimum, it will still present Jesus as predicting a time of trouble after His departure that includes the downfall of Jerusalem and the ruin of the temple. Furthermore, the bulk of Jesus' teaching presupposes a continuing society. In view of this preparation for the future, is it not somewhat precarious to assume that the disciples went ahead and, contrary to all instruction, fabricated the doctrine of an immediate return?[5]

---

4 It is interesting that since *The Apostolic Preaching* Dodd seems to have altered his position on this point. In *Gospel and Law* (written some fifteen years later) he says that "the extent to which that belief [the winding up of history] prevailed has perhaps been exaggerated, but some early Christians certainly held it" (pp. 27-28).

5 In *The Coming of Christ* (1954) Dodd admits that Jesus contemplated a further period of history after His departure and prepared His disciples for it (p. 17). It seems to me that this concession under-

(3) When treating New Testament verses that seem to reflect an air of imminence, we must always keep in mind the Semitic love of paradox. It is characteristically Jewish to throw together two extreme statements with the intention that they should qualify each other. It is quite wrong to interpret one half of the paradox in isolation. It should also be remembered that in a passage like Romans 13:11-14, "imminence" may be more of a rhetorical device to stimulate earnestness than a bald declaration of an immediate return.[6]

A second point in Dodd's reconstruction that needs to be contested is his unfavorable interpretation of those New Testament documents that develop a "futuristic" eschatology. II Thessalonians, for example, is understood as an attempt to explain the delay in the *Parousia* by reverting to the materials of apocalyptic eschatology. Dodd holds that this development was contrary to the best interests of Christianity and threatened to lead it back ultimately to a denial of the substance of the Gospel.[7]

The section especially in question is II Thessalonians 2:3-10, whose underlying motive is said to be the problem as to why the Lord had not yet come. But is this, in fact, the case? A careful reading of the text will show that the element of disturbance was not delay in His coming, but false reports that the day of the Lord had already come. Paul pauses in the middle of this very section in which he is setting forth the events that must precede the second Advent and asks, "Do you not remember that when I was still with you I told you this?" (v. 5).[8] It appears that the Thessalonians had forgotten Paul's

mines his whole concept of the development of the *kerygma*. If the disciples were prepared for the interval, then we cannot logically speak of an "unexpected delay." But without an "unexpected delay" the crux of the argument has been removed.

6 G. S. Duncan (*Jesus, Son of Man*, p. 256) suggests that the imminence of the *Parousia* should be understood, not in terms of *time*, but in the sense that, in view of certain things that had happened, the coming was seen to be certain.

7 Dodd, *The Apostolic Preaching*, p. 40.

8 This verse flatly contradicts Dodd's claim that Paul introduced II Thess. 2:3-10 as an "afterthought of which he had said nothing in his preaching" (*Apostolic Preaching*, p. 31).

instruction, and when rumors began to fly to the effect that the Day had already come, they became not a little excited. This is the situation to which Paul writes in his second letter.

Equally questionable is the interpretation of the situation reflected in I Thessalonians. Dodd holds that Paul had expressed himself in such unqualified terms that his converts were surprised and bewildered when certain of their number died before the expected Advent.[9] But is this not fitting facts to the theory? Where, in either the text or the context of Paul's words on the coming resurrection (I Thess. 4:13 – 5:11), is the slightest indication that it was occasioned by any upset expectations of an immediate Advent? It is much more likely that the mourning that Paul sets out to correct was due to the preconversion influences of paganism. Certain converts were grieving as did those who had no hope, so Paul explains the Christian doctrine of resurrection, both by way of encouragement (5:11) and so that they might not fail to command the respect of outsiders (4:12).

Thus, while the Thessalonian correspondence is strongly eschatological, it nowhere supports the view that the converts were wrestling with the problem of a delay and had to be put right by Paul, who, having salvaged the ancient myth of Belial, explained that the Son of Perdition must first be revealed.

A final objection to Dodd's view is his failure to provide an adequate explanation for the lingering elements of futurism in Paul and John. For example, when we examine Philippians (which, according to Dodd, was probably the final Epistle from the pen of St. Paul)[10] we three times find reference to the coming "day of [Jesus] Christ" (1:6, 10, 2:14). This is to be the day when all creation will confess His Lordship (2:10-11); the dead in Christ shall rise (3:11), and those who await His coming will be changed into His glorious likeness (3:20-21). "Rejoice," exclaims Paul, "the Lord is at hand" (4:4-5). If Paul, in his later letters, was intent on explaining the "delay" in terms of Christ-mysticism as over against futuristic escha-

9 Dodd, *New Testament Studies*, p. 110.
10 *Ibid.*, p. 108.

tology, how is it that he included so much material which would have encouraged and perpetuated the error?

How, then, is the *kerygma* related to the rest of the New Testament? What is the nature of the development involved? We will be a long way towards the answer if we remember that, while the *kerygma* is proclamation to a non-Christian audience for the purpose of evangelization, the bulk of the New Testament is instruction for Christians with a view toward spiritual growth. To relate the two on the same level is to blur their distinctive qualities. We must, therefore, not think of the development of the *kerygma* in terms of lineal progression (from the crude and eschatological to the refined and mystical), but in terms of theological and ethical expansion. It is not that the *kerygma* undergoes any significant alteration, but that the unique event which by it is interpreted for missionary purposes, also carries vast implications for Christian living, and the drawing out of these implications constitutes the development which we find in the New Testament.

It is helpful to visualize the New Testament materials as forming three concentric circles around the death, resurrection, and exaltation of Christ. The first circle is the *kerygma*, which interprets these events with a view to bringing men to faith in Christ. The second circle is the theological expansion of the first. Its purpose is to lead the new believer into a fuller apprehension of what God has accomplished through Christ Jesus. The outside circle is the ethical expansion of the other two. It lays hold on this new relationship of man to God and brings it into focus for practical daily living.

Defining development in terms of theological and ethical expansion, let us now investigate the particular contributions of various New Testament writers.

THE TEACHING OF PETER

We turn first to Peter, not as if he were the first apostle to set pen to papyrus,[11] but because his writing "does undoubtedly reflect the tradition and teaching of the primitive

---

11 The traditonal dating of I Peter (A.D. 63-64) places it later than the bulk of the Pauline material.

Church with a sympathy and sensitiveness unequaled in any other Epistle."[12] Our primary task is to show the relationship between his Epistle (written in the darkening shadows of persecution by way of encouragement and instruction) and the missionary proclamation of the primitive Church. To what extent does the *kerygma* form the substratum of his teaching, and in what sense does he expand or develop it for his particular purpose? These questions can be most effectively answered by discussing the thought of the apostle against the background of the reconstructed *kerygma*.

It will be remembered that the *kerygma* began with a proclamation of the death, resurrection, and exaltation of Jesus.

Comparing I Peter and the *kerygma* in reference to the death of Christ, one is immediately struck by the remarkable number of similarities between the two.[13] Both refer to the death of Christ in terms of suffering (cf. I Pet. 1:11, Acts 3:18). In both cases this suffering is seen as the fulfillment of prophecy. The degradation of the crucifixion (He was hung "upon a tree") [14] is a characteristic item in both *kerygma* and Epistle (Acts 5:30, 10:39, I Pet. 2:24). Both portray Christ as the Servant of God (Acts 3:13, 26, I Pet. 2:22-25) whose death had a vicarious and atoning significance (I Cor. 15:3, I Pet. 2:24, 3:18). Both vividly contrast Christ's rejection by man with His exaltation by God (Acts 4:10-11, I Pet. 2:4, 7).[15]

Peter, however, shows a definite advance over the *kerygma*. Not only was Christ the Suffering Servant who gave His life for the many (2:21), but He was also the Paschal Lamb whose shed blood was the ransom that delivered man from the bondage of sin (1:18-19).[16] If I Peter 2:24 is an allusion to Leviti-

---

12 E. G. Selwyn, *The First Epistle of St. Peter*, p. 32.

13 If the speeches in Acts and the Epistle are both genuinely Petrine (although in one instance Luke was the editor, and in the other Silvanus the amanuensis) this is what we should expect.

14 Cf. Deut. 21:23.

15 This contrast occurs in every early speech in Acts: 2:23-24, 3:13-14, 4:10-11, 5:30, and 10:39-40.

16 The blood of Christ is also set forth as the means by which men's sins are covered so that they may enter into covenant with God (1:2).

cus 16:20ff., then Christ is also pictured as the Scapegoat who carries away the iniquities of the people.

The distinctive thing about Peter's treatment of the death of Christ, however, is not his expansion of its significance by way of illustration, but the practical use to which he puts it. For Peter, the manner in which Christ suffered is the supreme example of how Christians are to meet suffering. He who committed no sin and upon whose lips was found no guile, in suffering unjustly for the sins of others, left for all His followers the perfect pattern of Christian meekness (2:21ff.). "Since therefore Christ suffered in the flesh," exhorts Peter, "arm yourselves with the same thought" (4:1). At this point theology begins to merge into ethics. It is only those who fail to see this extremely close relationship who charge Peter with teaching an "exemplarist view" of the atonement. The valid Christian ethic has its roots deep in the Cross.

But how does Peter's teaching differ from the Stoic doctrine of the subordination of the individual? The answer is that it goes on to affirm the striking paradox of "joy in suffering." Suffering is not to be borne with grim determination, but with an exalted and unutterable joy (1:8). How can this be? It is because suffering not only strengthens faith, but it ultimately leads to "praise and glory and honor" (1:6-7). "Down in the Alpine valley it is still dark, but those who will look up to the mountain peaks can already see the light of the new day and can live the remainder of the time of darkness in its strength and joy."[17] Furthermore, suffering may be within the will of God (3:17, 4:19), and a sharing of the sufferings of Christ (4:13).

In speaking of the resurrection, Peter maintains (as did the *kerygma*) that it was God who raised Jesus from the dead (Acts 2:24, I Pet. 1:21). This resurrection brought about new birth to a living hope, an inheritance of "fellowship with God undimmed by sin."[18]

When we examine Peter's thought concerning the exaltation, we see that he links it together with the sufferings of

17 C. E. B. Cranfield, *The First Epistle of Peter*, p. 28.
18 *Ibid.*, p. 24.

Christ as being one of the twin themes of Old Testament prophecy (1:11). In both I Peter and the *kerygma* it is represented as an act of God (Acts 3:13, I Pet. 1:21) whereby Christ is given to sit at the right hand of the Father (Acts 2:33, 5:31, I Pet. 3:22). Peter goes on a bit further, however, when he speaks of the resultant subjection of heavenly beings (3:22).

Having said that Peter saw the death and exaltation of Jesus as the fulfillment of prophecy, we must now inquire further concerning his understanding of eschatology. Can we detect an advance in his outlook over that of the primitive *kerygma?*

Selwyn answers that the eschatology of I Peter "stands in that central tradition of New Testament teaching for which eschatology is for the most part eschatology fulfilled."[19] This is a valid observation. For Peter, the incarnation was an eschatological event (1:20). The end had drawn near (4:7) and judgment had begun with the household of God (4:17). Yet, at the same time, he looks forward to the final consummation. This culminating event is called the "revelation [not *parousia*] of Jesus Christ" (1:7, 13). It will be a time when the glory of Christ will be manifested (4:13) and the faithful will receive an unfading crown of glory (5:4). Salvation in all its completeness will also be revealed in this "last time" (1:5), and the unrighteous will meet judgment (4:5, 17).[20]

We judge, therefore, that in both I Peter and the *kerygma* eschatology is both realized and futurist. Chronologically, the present is preparation for the future: theologically, the future governs and conditions the present.[21]

We found that the second part of the *kerygma* consisted in a theological evaluation of the One who had been crucified by man but raised and exalted by God. I Peter displays the same elevated view of the risen Christ as did the *kerygma*. It is only through Him that man can arrive at an adequate faith in God (1:21). While there are many titles that may be ap-

---

19 Selwyn, "Eschatology in I Peter," *The Background of the New Testament and Its Eschatology,* p. 399.

20 The term "day of visitation" (2:12) probably refers in this context to the crisis of salvation rather than the day of Judgment. Cf. Beyer in *Theologisches Wörterbuch zum Neuen Testament,* II, 604.

21 Selwyn, *The First Epistle of St. Peter,* p. 112.

plied to Him,[22] He is pre-eminently the One to whom the name given to Yahweh in the Old Testament can be supplied — He is the *Lord* (2:3, 13, 3:15).

Since I Peter is not a public proclamation of Christianity designed to bring men to faith, but a letter of instruction and encouragement to those living as God-fearers in the hostility of a pagan environment (4:3-4),[23] we would not expect it to include a call to repentance. It is interesting, though, to note that its view of the non-Christian world is one which implies the necessity of repentance.[24]

THE TEACHING OF PAUL

It will not be necessary for our present purpose to relate the entire theological thought of Paul to the message of the primitive Church. Sufficient insight into the manner in which he expands the *kerygma* can be gained by centering our attention on his two most distinctive theological contributions.

The first is in the field of soteriology. It is almost unnecessary to remind ourselves of the centrality of the Cross in the thought of Paul. "Far be it from me to glory," he exclaims, "except in the cross of our Lord Jesus Christ" (Gal. 6:14). The death of Christ was the subject of Paul's most profound reflection. Little wonder then that he seems to invade every sphere of life in search of analogies that will somehow express the inexhaustible significance of the Cross. It is an exhibition of the love of God (Rom. 5:8, 8:32-39), a victory over the demonic powers of evil (Col. 2:15), a sacrifice for sin (I Cor. 5:7, Eph. 5:2), a free gift (Rom. 8:32) that brings forgiveness (I Cor. 15:17, Eph. 1:7).

To express the salvation that it accomplishes, Paul uses the suggestive terms redemption, justification, and reconciliation.

22 Living Stone (2:4), Sinless One (2:22), Servant (2:22-25), Chief Shepherd (5:4), etc.
23 I believe that Professor van Unnik ("Christianity According to I Peter," *Expository Times*, LXVIII [Dec. 1956], 79-83) has proved that Peter is not here speaking of formal persecution but of sufferings that come from ill-tempered neighbors (p. 80).
24 They are said to live in "licentiousness, passions, drunkenness, revels, carousing, and lawless idolatry . . . wild profligacy" (4:3-4). Cf. also 1:14, 18, 2:9.

The first pictures an enslaved man being set free[25] ("Christ *redeemed* us from the curse of the law" — Gal. 3:13), the second, a guilty man being acquitted ("All who believe . . . are *justified* by his grace as a gift" — Rom. 3:22-24), and the third, an estranged child being taken back into his parent's favor ("God . . . through Christ *reconciled* us to himself" — II Cor. 5:18). Paul has taken over the rough diamond of the kerygmatic "Christ died for our sins" and, as a master crafts-man, has polished it by meditation until now its inherent brilliance is released through a thousand facets. It is still the same saving fact that Peter proclaimed at Pentecost, but now its implications for theology and life have been brought sharply into focus.

The most distinctive contribution in connection with Paul's theological expansion of the *kerygma* is his solving of the problem of salvation in terms of "justification by faith." To the agelong question, How can a man get right with God?, Paul gives the resounding answer, "He who through faith is righteous shall live" (Gal. 3:11).

Behind Paul's doctrine lies the Old Testament concept of righteousness. The Hebrew words *tsedeq* and *tsedaqah*, while originally signifying that which conforms to the character of God,[26] came to be interpreted in terms of active benevolence or salvation. Thus, in a passage like Isaiah 51:5:

> My righteousness is near;
> my salvation is gone forth

the two concepts are virtually synonymous. The important point is that the righteousness of God was understood, not as a static idea, but as a dynamic force. It was God's grace in action for the vindication of His purposes with all mankind, and especially with Israel.

But what of the times when God failed to intervene? The only answer is that Israel had been in the wrong. This led to the conclusion that God's righteousness (in the sense of divine pronouncement) must in some way be bound up with man's

25 These "picture phrases" are developed in A. M. Hunter's *Inter-preting Paul's Gospel*, pp. 23ff.

26 Karl Barth (*Epistle to the Romans*, p. 40) explains righteousness as "the consistency of God with himself."

obedience. The resulting tension afforded Pharisaic Judaism the opportunity to expand upon man's obligations. The end product was a vast labyrinth of legalism designed to instruct man how to influence, if not determine, God's final verdict. When all was said and done, God would acquit or pronounce righteous the man whose good deeds merited salvation.

It was this belief in "righteousness by works" that drove Paul relentlessly on. But instead of rewarding him, it exposed his sinfulness. Instead of issuing in peace, it drove him to despair. It was a mirage that beckoned, but, like all mirages, deceived.

Then the unbelievable happened. Christ met Paul on the road to Damascus. From this dramatic encounter in which *God* had taken the initiative, Paul began to grasp the revolutionary truth that righteousness is not the product of strenuous moral endeavor, but a free gift of the grace of God. It cannot be earned; it can only be accepted. Kennedy has rightly said that "the supreme wonder of Paul's conversion-crisis was that there God took the initiative."[27]

Righteousness, then, is to be understood as a new status conferred upon all those who respond in faith to the self-disclosure of God in Christ Jesus. Man's part is simply to receive it by faith. "To one who does not work but trusts him who justifies the ungodly, his faith is reckoned as righteousness" (Rom. 4:5).

The *kerygma* declared that Christ "died for our sins." Paul grasps this basic truth and relates it more broadly to man's universal longing for divine acquittal. Paul declares to all men everywhere, not, "The just shall obtain life as the reward of his faithfulness" but, "He who is just by faith shall live."[28]

Paul's second contribution was in the field of Christology. The *kerygma* had proclaimed that Jesus of Nazareth was both Lord and Christ (Acts 2:36). Paul eagerly seized the first title and into it poured the wealth of his own devotion. While granting to Jesus the most exalted religous significance, it also portrayed Paul's own status as bond-slave. The title "Messiah,"

27 H. A. A. Kennedy, *The Theology of the Epistles,* p. 133.
28 J. Jeremias, "Paul and James," *Expository Times,* LXVI (Sept. 1955), 369.

on the other hand, because it would be meaningless in Gentile ears, was rarely used by Paul except as a personal name.

Other Messianic titles ("Servant," "Holy One," etc.) also passed into disuse because the significance of Jesus could no longer be expressed in terms of a national expectation.[29] It had broken the temporary mold of Messianism and demanded new and more comprehensive categories. Thus Paul describes Christ as the Last Adam (I Cor. 15:45ff.), the Wisdom of God (I Cor. 1:24, 30) and the New Torah (Rom. 10:6ff.).

Here again Paul is ransacking language and thought in an attempt to express more adequately the absolute significance of Christ. It is not surprising then that sooner or later we should find him relating his Lord to the entire order of created things. This he does in Colossians 1:15-20.

Here Paul sets forth Christ as the "image of the invisible God, the first-born of all creation." While nature reflects certain aspects of God (Rom. 1:20), Christ is His perfect likeness.[30] That He is "first-born of all creation" means that He is both prior to and supreme over all created things. This is because He is the conditioning cause ("*in* him"), the mediating agent ("*through* him"), and the appointed goal ("*for* him") of their very existence. His absolute existence[31] necessarily places Him before all creation. In fact, it is in Him that all things cohere. Ultimately He will reconcile to Himself, by virtue of His atoning death, the totality of all creation.

The question that immediately confronts us concerns the source of Paul's cosmic vocabulary. Some have turned to Alexandrian Judaism and the Logos doctrine of Philo.[32] Others

29 The title "Son of God" could be carried over because although originally Messianic (V. Taylor, *The Names of Jesus*, p. 70), it quite appropriately signified to the Greek mind a supernatural being (p. 54). The uniqueness of this "Son" is emphasized by Paul in verses like Rom. 8:32 and Gal. 4:4-5.

30 εἰκών not ὁμοίωμα.

31 Reading αὐτός ἐστιν (v. 17) and understanding ἐστίν in light of John 8:58 ("before Abraham was, ἐγώ εἰμι ") rather than taking it as a mere copula. Cf. C. F. D. Moule, *The Epistles to the Colossians and to Philemon (Cambridge Greek New Testament Commentary)*, pp. 66-67.

32 J. Weiss, *The History of Primitive Christianity*, II 482ff.; J. B. Lightfoot, *The Epistles of St. Paul: Colossians and Philemon*, pp. 141ff.

have searched out a number of analogies in the literature of Stoicism.[33] Still others have linked Paul's language more closely with the particular heresy that was threatening the Colossian church.[34] While the philosophical speculation and religious syncretism of the age undoubtedly influenced Paul's vocabulary to some extent, it is hard to deny the cogency of Rawlinson's argument that for Paul to have consciously depended upon what he himself would have described as the "wisdom of this world," is unthinkable.[35]

A much likelier source is the Wisdom literature of Judaism. Here we meet the figure of Wisdom (a personification born of the attempt to reconcile transcendence and immanence in the realms of creation, and otherwise)[36], who is pictured as not only being pre-existent, but also, in some sense, an agent in creation.[37] These are the very attributes that Paul assigns to Christ in Colossians. For this reason and because modern scholarship is becoming increasingly aware of the extent of Paul's debt to Judaism, we may be fairly certain that here is the source that underlies Paul's description of Jesus in cosmological terms.[38]

To sum up, we may say that while the *kerygma* had expressed the essential significance of Jesus in terms of redemp-

33 Paul's "all coheres in" is said to reflect the Stoic belief in a World Soul — "the constitutive principle in the system of created things" (Kennedy, *op. cit.*, p. 155). Eduard Norden (*Agnostos Theos*, pp. 240-50) emphasizes the affinities of Paul's language (especially the prepositional phrases) with the current philosophical thought.

34 E. F. Scott (*Colossians* in the *Moffatt N. T. Commentary*) says, in connection with the term πλήρωμα (fullness), that Paul "borrows from the heretics their favorite catch-word, and keeps turning it against them" (p. 26).

35 A. E. J. Rawlinson, *The New Testament Doctrine of the Christ*, p. 164.

36 Cf. Dodd, *The Authority of the Bible*, pp. 178f.

37 "When he marked out the foundation of the earth, then I was beside him, like a master workman" (Prov. 8:29b-30).

38. This is worked out in detail by W. D. Davies in chapter 7 of *Paul and Rabbinic Judaism* ("The Old and the New Torah: Christ the Wisdom of God," pp. 147-76). The link between Jesus and Wisdom in the mind of Paul is shown to be his conception of Christ as a New Torah (pp. 162ff.).

tion and sovereignty, Paul added a third dimension — Jesus was also the pre-existent Agent of creation whose death for sins would ultimately reconcile all things to Himself, whether on earth or in heaven.

THE TEACHING OF THE AUTHOR OF HEBREWS

Upon turning to the book of Hebrews, we are immediately aware of having moved into a quite different atmosphere. No longer do we hear Paul's constant reminders that we are "justified by faith" or Peter's emphasis on the "exemplary" value of Christ's death. Our new world is one that abounds with the language of priestly ritual. We sit at the feet of one who seized upon the idealist element in apocalyptic and, in terms that speculative philosophy could appreciate, presented the high-priesthood of Christ as the great ministry by which men are enabled to achieve the *summum bonum* of religion — access to God.

Does this mean that the *kerygma* has been left behind in the interest of commending the Christian faith to a wider audience? Not at all. While the external form of presentation has altered, the basic core is still God's redemptive act in Christ Jesus. The primitive message can be shown to be remarkably complete in this work that seems to be engaged so strongly in a different pursuit.[39]

What concerns us here, however, is the way in which the *kerygma* is developed by the author.[40] His distinctive contributions lie along three lines.

In the first place, he interprets the person and work of Christ in terms of priestly ritual and sacrifice. The analogy he draws is from the ministry of the Levitical high priest, who on the Day of Atonement offered sacrifice on behalf of the people and then, taking the blood that bore witness to this purification, entered behind the veil and stood for a brief interval in the presence of God. This act renewed the cove-

---

39 Cf. A. M. Hunter, *Introducing New Testament Theology*, pp. 119-20.

40 Since the authorship of Hebrews has baffled the Christian Church from Origen to the present day, we shall settle for the non-committal *"Auctor ad Hebraeos,"* and suggest that he was not unlike the Alexandrian Jew described in Acts 18:24ff.

nant and allowed Israel to maintain her status as God's chosen people.

Against this background, the author presents Christ as the ideal High Priest (8:1) who, having offered the perfect sacrifice (9:26, 10:14), entered into the true sanctuary (9:24) where He ministers forever on our behalf (7:24-25). As to His person, He is the true High Priest of whose ministry the Levitical priesthood had been only prelude and symbol. He is superior because of His divine ordination (5:4-6) and His unique ability to sympathize and help (2:14-18, 4:14-16). Like Melchizedek, His priesthood stems from an inherent worthiness; it is not the result of a genealogical accident (7:15-16). As to His sacrifice, it is the one true offering that puts away sin (9:26), perfects the believer (10:14), and purifies the conscience (9:14). It inaugurates the New Covenant whereby God provides for man access into a new and immeasurably more intimate relationship (8:8-12). The sacrifice of Christ enables the human spirit to pass out of the sphere of death and find its real home in the sphere of God.[41] As to His present ministry, He ever lives to make intercession on our behalf (7:25). He is the new and living way whereby man can now with confidence draw near unto God (10:19-20).

A second distinctive contribution of the author is his emphasis upon access to God as the essence of true religion (4:16, 7:19, 25, 10:22, 12:22-24). His entire doctrine of the priesthood of Christ is presented as the answer to man's agelong religious dilemma. If the material world with its institutions is but a shadowy representation of the invisible realm of perfect reality, then what man needs for salvation is access to the higher sphere where God is. The proper approach is through acceptable worship, but this is ever hindered by sin. The problem becomes, How can this defilement be removed?

The Old Testament institution of sacrifice pointed in the right direction, but proved inadequate. Being external and symbolic, it could only offer ritual purification. In order to perfect the conscience of the worshipper it was necessary that

41 Kennedy, *op. cit.*, p. 214.

the temporary and typical be replaced by the abiding and real. Thus the author presents the death of Christ as the archetype of the Levitical offering — the one perfect sacrifice that purifies the conscience from its sense of guilt and thereby grants the confidence to draw near unto God.

The *kerygma* had promised the forgiveness of sins (Acts 2:38, 10:43) and the gift of the Holy Spirit (Acts 2:38, 5:32). It also understood that with the death of Christ the New Covenan had been inaugurated (I Cor. 11:25). This nexus of primitive ideas was taken up by the author of Hebrews and rephrased in terms of access to God. In this way he related the *kerygma* more broadly to the religious aspirations of all mankind.

The author's third contribution is his use of philosophical terminology in the presentation of Christian truth. In the prologue he speaks of Christ as the "effulgence" (ἀπαύγασμα) of God's glory and the "impress" (χαρακτήρ) of His essence (1:3). These terms most certainly reflect the philosophical atmosphere of Alexandrian Judaism.[42] So also does the two-story view of reality, which at least one modern writer judges to be the controlling thought of the entire Epistle.[43] Other similarities to Alexandrian thought are the author's love of allegory, the broad (and un-Pauline) definition of faith a "confident reliance upon the reality of the unseen and immaterial," and a certain similarity between the Christology of Hebrews and Philo's doctrine of the Logos.[44]

At this point, however, we must exercise a certain restraint. While there are similarities between the author and Philo, there are also marked differences. For Philo, the Logos is a personified abstraction whose mediation consists in the communication of the divine nature as it exists in Reason. This

42 In the Alexandrian *Wisdom of Solomon*, the heavenly Wisdom is depicted as the ἀπαύγασμα of everlasting light (vii. 25, 26). Philo refers to the Logos as the χαρακτήρ of the seal of God (*De Plantat.*, 18).
43 A. C. Purdy, *The Epistle to the Hebrews* (Interpreter's Bible, XI, 584).
44 Cf. E. F. Scott (*The Epistle to the Hebrews*, pp. 163-64) for a convenient comparison.

is entirely foreign to the author, who presents Christ as a real and living person who effects actual cleansing from sin.

It should also be noted that the entire imagery of the heavenly sanctuary and its ministrations does not find its origin in the idealism of Plato, but in the eschatological temple of apocalyptic Judaism.[45] Nor does the doctrine of the priesthood of Christ arise from Philonic speculation about a heavenly priest. It finds its origin in the "charter-document of the writer's Christology" — the 110th Psalm.[46]

These observations lead to the conclusion that while the basic themes of Hebrews arise from within the literature of Judaism, they are nevertheless presented in a manner not incompatible with the terminology of philosophic idealism. The author differs from Plato in that "the shadows in his cave are all shadows of an event that happened once for all, the death of Jesus."[47] As long as this eschatological priority is maintained, "Hebrews itself, as part of the N. T. canon, shows that the language of philosophy may be more serviceable in expressing Christian truth than some Biblical theologians are prepared to allow."[48]

THE TEACHING OF JOHN

Among the writers of the New Testament, none offers a more profound interpretation of the essential meaning of Christ than does the author of the Fourth Gospel.[49] We shall here attempt only to sketch several characteristic ways in which John expands the *kerygma* of the apostolic Church.

Perhaps the most distinctive contribution of John in this connection is his emphasis on what has come to be known as

45 This point is made quite forcibly by C. K. Barrett in his article "The Eschatology of the Epistle to the Hebrews" (*The Background of the New Testament and its Eschatology*, esp. pp. 374-75, 383-90, 393) .

46 W. Manson, *The Epistle to the Hebrews*, pp. 117-121.

47 Barrett, *op. cit.*, p. 393.

48 *Ibid., loc. cit.*

49 It is maintained that the Fourth Evangelist is also the author of the Johannine Epistles. The apocalyptic nature of the book of Revelation places it apart from what is commonly accepted as distinctively Johannine.

"realized eschatology." It will be remembered that the early
evangelists proclaimed the death, resurrection, and exaltation
of Christ against the background of fulfilled prophecy. While
their particular task was to bring men to faith in the risen
Lord rather than to discourse on the dispensational change He
effected, they nevertheless were very much aware that with the
outpouring of the Spirit the Messianic Age had in some sense
been inaugurated. With acute spiritual insight John develops
the implications of this truth in at least three different direc-
tions:

(1) If the Age to Come has invaded the present, then the
life of the New Age ("eternal life") can be a present possession. Thus John writes, "He who believes in the Son *has*
eternal life" (John 3:36); "He who has the Son *has* life"
(I John 5:12). Eternal life (John's major concern) is no
flickering hope for the future, but a blessed reality to be
possessed here and now.

(2) But if a man is already living in eternity, then judgment must also be realized. This finds expression in the
words, "He who hears my word and believes him who sent
me . . . does not come into judgment, but has passed from
death to life" (John 5:24). The corollary is that the unbe-
liever is living now under condemnation (John 3:18).

(3) A third eschatological concept that John "contemporizes"[50] is resurrection. Without refuting Martha's orthodox
hope that her brother would "rise again in the resurrection at
the last day," Jesus adds the startling statement, "I am the
resurrection and the life" (John 11:24-25). To the Jews at
Jerusalem He proclaims, "The hour is coming, and now is,
when the [spiritually] dead will hear . . . and live" (John 5:25).

This strong emphasis on the realization of eschatological
realities has led some to maintain that John "de-eschatologizes"
the Gospel and offers us instead a semi-Platonic Christian mysti-
cism. But this is to ignore his straightforward teaching concerning the final denouement of history. There will be, he

50 This term is used quite effectively by G. E. Ladd in an article,
"Eschatology and the Unity of New Testament Theology," *Expository
Times*, LXVIII (June 1957), 268-73.

says, a "last day" in which Christ shall return (John 14:3, 21: 22, I John 2:28), the dead shall be raised (John 6:39, 40, 44, 54), and final judgment pronounced (John 5:29, 12:48, I John 4:17). John may well have refined away some of the "crudely eschatological elements" in the primitive outlook, but he by no means vaporized the truth they were intended to convey. To find the fulfillment of Christ's promise to return in His resurrection and the coming of the Paraclete[51] may satisfy certain verses (such as John 14:18, 16:16), but fails to do justice to others (John 14:3, 21:22, I John 2:28). And it will not do to maintain that the eschatological terminology and apocalyptic imagery of John are "concessions" to popular thought that "obscure the characteristic teaching of the Gospel."[52]

The total evidence requires us to conclude that, while developing the truth of "realized eschatology," John does not abandon the eschatological tension that characterized the Christian *Weltanschauung*. Along with the other New Testament writers, he holds that there is a "not yet," as well as a "now."[53] The paradox of tenses that is so clearly seen in John's "the hour cometh and now is" (John 4:23, 5:25), is a result of trying to describe the entrance into history of the "absolute" or "supra-historical" in terms of temporal eschatology.[54]

A second Johannine contribution to the development of the primitive faith is John's unfolding of the unique Sonship of Jesus. It is this theme that reveals his most profound thought about Christ.

Although the speeches in Acts do not actually refer to Jesus as the "Son of God," by calling Him Messiah they have said approximately the same thing. John now takes over this Mes-

51 Cf. Dodd, *The Apostolic Preaching*, pp. 66, 73; *The Johannine Epistles* (Moffatt Series), p. xxxv. In *The Coming of Christ* (1954), Dodd speaks of Christ "coming" in the Eucharist (p. 9), at death (p. 28), in the recurrent crises of history (p. 32), and finally, *beyond* history (p. 16). His coming "in history," however, was fulfilled by the post-resurrection appearances (p. 14).

52 E. F. Scott, *The Fourth Gospel*, p. 249.

53 Edwyn Bevan, *Symbolism and Belief*, p. 117n.

54 C. K. Barrett, *The Gospel According to St. John*, p. 56.

sianic terminology of the early Church — but not without redefining its content.[55] It was impossible that any existing
label should do justice to his expanding appreciation of the
significance of Christ. What John has to say about Jesus as
the Son of God may be summarized as follows:

(1) The divine Sonship of Jesus is unique and unshared
(John 1:14, 18, 3:16, 18, I John 4:9). One aspect of this
uniqueness is the unbroken filial unity which He shares with
the Father (10:30, 17:21). This relationship is expressed in
terms of loving confidence on the part of the Father (John
3:55) and obedient trust on the part of the Son (John 8:29,
18:11). Because of this moral likeness and essential identity,
the Son is the perfect revealer of the Father (John 1:18). To
know the Son is to know the Father (John 8:19, 14:9).

(2) The Sonship of Jesus is patterned after the model of
the ideal prophet of the Old Testament economy.[56] Throughout the Gospel, Jesus is set forth as one who has been "sent"
by the Father, who acts in strict subordination, and to whom
authority over mankind has been delegated.

(3) As the Son of God, Jesus exercises two supreme preroga-
tives: first, the giving of life (John 5:21, 10:10) and secondly,
the executing of judgment (John 5:22, 27, 30). These are
really two sides of the same divine activity. To fail to respond
to the revelation of light in Christ is to place oneself under
condemnation (John 3:19).

(4) Finally, Jesus does not become Son by virtue of miraculous conception or rebirth, but belongs by nature to a higher
sphere (John 8:23). It is divine origin that we meet in the
claim, "I came from the Father and have come into the world"
(John 16:28).

Two other areas of Johannine development should be noted.
The first has to do with John's theological expansion of the
simple kerygmatic claim that repentance and obedience will be
rewarded by the gift of the Holy Spirit (Acts 5:32). Peter

55 Vincent Taylor (*The Names of Jesus,* p. 70) notes that when the
Fourth Evangelist writes, "These are written that you may believe that
Jesus is the Christ, the Son of God" (20:31), "all that is left of Jewish
Messianic teaching is the language."

56 Dodd, *The Interpretation of the Fourth Gospel,* pp. 254-55.

understood the spectacular activity of the day of Pentecost to be the fulfillment of Joel's prophecy that in the last days God would pour out His Spirit (Acts 2:16ff.) · But it remained for John to formulate the exact nature of the Spirit's ministry.[57] This he does most fully in the five Paraclete sayings. The Helper is to come as Christ's *Alter Ego* (14:15-17) to continue the work of the Son (14:25-26) · As the Spirit of truth, He will proceed from the Father and bear witness to the Son (15:26-27) · He will contemporize the issues of eschatological judgment (16:5-11) and guide the course of revelation to its consummate goal (16:12-15).

The other area concerns John's choice of terminology. The immediate reaction to his opening statement, "In the beginning was the Logos," is to suspect that we are about to read a completely Hellenized version of the Christian Gospel. Is this not the very term that Philo used so extensively (over 1300 times) to indicate "the personified activity of God in creation and redemption"? Our suspicions seem almost confirmed when we note John's flair for the Hellenistic contrast between light and darkness (John 1:4f., 1 John 2:8ff.), his understanding of truth as "reality,"[58] and his emphasis on mediation between God and man.

Here again, however, we must remember that while there are certain similarities between the thought and vocabulary of the later New Testament writers and that of philosophical Hellenism, there are also distinct differences. For example, if a pagan were to read the Prologue to the Fourth Gospel, he would realize by the time he reached verse 14 ("and the Logos became flesh") that it could never have come from the pen of Philo. While John borrows, to some extent, the vocabulary of Hellenism, he reinterprets it in terms of the incarnation. The roots of his thought lie deep in Jewish soil.[59]

57 "The Johannine teaching about the Holy Spirit is one of the most distinctive features of the Gospel" (W. F. Howard, *Christianity According to St. John*, pp. 71-72).

58 Cf. Dodd, *op. cit.*, pp. 174-78.

59 For a convenient list of some of the parallels between the Fourth Gospel and the Old Testament, see W. F. Howard's introduction to *The Gospel According to St. John* (*Interpreter's Bible*, VIII, 456).

To bridge the gap between a Semitic Gospel and a non-Semitic audience is a problem almost as old as Christianity itself. John has laid all subsequent interpreters in his debt by indicating the correct approach by which this cultural and linguistic barrier may be overcome.

SUMMARY

These, then, are the lines along which the early Church gradually developed the primitive *kerygma*. Peter enlarges upon the death of Christ as an example of how Christians are to meet suffering. Paul shows us that by virtue of this death we may be justified by faith, and then goes on to extol the grandeur of Christ in relation to the entire order of created things. The author of Hebrews interprets the work of Christ in terms of priestly ritual and sacrifice, and emphasizes (with terminology not incompatible with philosophy) that access to God is the essence of true religion. Finally, John teaches us more about "realized eschatology," and with loving insight unfolds the unique Sonship of Christ.

It is not that the *kerygma* itself underwent any basic change, but that it provided a source for new and profound meditation concerning the nature and activity of God. The great redemptive act of God in Christ Jesus remains central. In the missionary *kerygma* it is proclaimed and men are brought to faith in Christ. In the didactic sections of the New Testament its theological and ethical implications are pondered, and the worshipping Church grows in the grace and knowledge of its Lord and Savior.

Chapter Nine

THE ESSENTIAL NATURE OF PREACHING

ONE of the distinctive gains of contemporary theological thought is that it has cleared the ground for a new appraisal of the vital significance of preaching. This has come about by the almost unexpected convergence of several current lines of thought, the more important being the rediscovery of the apostolic *kerygma*, a redefining of the concept of revelation, and a new grasp on the centrality of the "I-Thou" relationship. No longer can we consider preaching to be just another medium for the communication of Christian doctrine. Nor can we any longer discuss it according to the general laws which govern all propaganda alike. The present situation demands that we investigate with renewed vigor the essential nature of the activity of preaching.

The phenomenon of preaching is best understood as it is related to the wider theme of revelation in general. Of recent years this has been the subject of much learned discussion. We have learned that while it is permissible to speak of all knowledge as "revealed," revelation, in the primary sense of the word, takes place only within the sphere of personal relationships. Properly understood, it is from subject to subject, and not of object to subject.[1]

We have also learned that what is revealed is not so much a body of information about the other person, as it is the person himself. Divine revelation is more than the disclosure of supranatural knowledge concerning the nature and purposes of God; "it is the self-disclosure of God Himself."[2] Many years ago P. T. Forsyth had grasped this truth when he wrote,

1 John Baillie, *The Idea of Revelation in Recent Thought*, p. 24.
2 Oepke, *Theologisches Wörterbuch zum Neuen Testament*, III, 586.

"Revelation is the self-bestowal of the living God . . . God in
the act of imparting Himself to living souls."[3]

A second fundamental insight into the theology of revelation
is that God reveals Himself *in action*. The Bible is essentially
a record of the acts of God. Its purpose is not to supply us
with a compendium of timeless truths, but to tell us what God
has done. It is not an unabridged collection of ethical and
religious maxims, but a chronicle of God's repeated interven-
tions on behalf of man. God reveals Himself in redemptive
activity, and this activity reaches its supreme climax in the
death and resurrection of Jesus Christ. It is here that God's
Self-disclosure bursts forth with unexcelled and unprecedented
clarity.

A third observation that emerges is that revelation, to be
complete, must be received. Revelation cannot take place in
a vacuum. There is no such thing as a true self-disclosure apart
from its apprehension by another. Archbishop Temple speaks
of revelation as consisting in "the intercourse of mind and
event."[4] Brunner concludes, "The fact of the illumination is
therefore an integral part of the process of revelation."[5]

And how is all this related to preaching? The connection
becomes clear when we realize that revelation and proclamation partake of the same nature. God reveals Himself in His
acts, we said. And is not the redemptive activity of God in
Christ Jesus the very heart of the *kerygma?* At this vital point,
revelation and proclamation become one. Preaching *is* revelation.

We went on to say that revelation is the interplay between
event and personal apprehension. It is incomplete without the
response of faith. Thus, the problem becomes, How can God
reveal Himself to me in the present through an event which
took place in the past? How can revelation, which by defini-

3 P. T. Forsyth, *Positive Preaching and the Modern Mind* (1907),
p. 10.
4 William Temple, *Nature, Man and God*, p. 315. Forsyth is making
the same point when he says, "Revelation is not revelation . . . till it
return to God in faith" (*op. cit.*, p. 235).
5 Emil Brunner, *Revelation and Reason*, p. 33.

tion is limited to the present, employ the once-for-all Self-disclosure of God in history?

The answer lies in the distinctive nature of preaching. As the preacher proclaims the divine act of redemption, the barriers of time are somehow transcended and that supreme event of the past is once again taking place. God's historic Self-disclosure has become a present actuality. John Knox has written:

> Preaching does more than recount and explain the ancient event. The Spirit makes the ancient event in a very real sense an event even now transpiring, and the preaching is a medium of the Spirit's action in doing so. In the preaching, when it is truly itself, the event is continuing or is recurring. God's revealing action in Christ is, still or again, actually taking place.[6]

"Preaching," declared Forsyth, is "the Gospel prolonging and declaring itself."[7]

Thus, preaching is that timeless link between God's great redemptive Act and man's apprehension of it. It is the medium through which God contemporizes His historic Self-disclosure and offers man the opportunity to respond in faith. Without response, revelation is incomplete. Without preaching, God's mighty act remains an event in the past. What man desperately needs is a redemptive encounter in the ever present Now. Preaching answers to this need by contemporizing the past and moving the individual to respond in faith. The contemporaneity of what took place long ago is an ultimate and inescapable miracle of Christianity. It defies explanation. Yet without this miracle, preaching is not really preaching.

This new understanding of the existential nature of preaching has necessitated a vigorous rethinking of the entire subject. It has led to a number of new and significant insights.

In the first place, preaching can no longer be considered as an adjunct (even an indispensable adjunct) to the saving activity of God in Christ. It is, rather, a part of that activity itself.[8] The proclamation of the Cross is itself the continu-

6 John Knox, *The Integrity of Preaching*, p. 92.
7 Forsyth, *op. cit.*, p. 3.
8 H. H. Farmer, *The Servant of the Word*, p. 21.

ance, or extension in time, of that very redemptive act. Professor Stewart writes, "The proclamation of the Word belongs itself to *Heilsgeschichte* as an integral part of God's continuous saving activity."[9] They are two phases of the one great act.

Secondly, we are now more aware that it is God Himself who speaks in the proclamation. Preaching is not talking *about* God; it is allowing *God* to talk.[10] The words of the preacher are simply the medium through which the Divine Word comes. It is God who speaks. This was what happened on the day of Pentecost. When the crowd heard the message, they were "cut to the heart." Why? Not because of any irresistible logic or persuasive oratory on the part of Peter, but because they had been confronted in judgment by God Himself.

A third gain is the realization that preaching is sacramental. This follows from the fact that in revelation it is God Himself who is communicated and not simply information about Him. Preaching is the "immediate, powerful, personal self-communication of the eternal Word to men."[11] It is therefore sacramental; it mediates the presence of God. "Preaching has a single purpose," writes Gustaf Wingren, "that Christ might come to those who have assembled to listen."[12]

In the fourth place, we now more correctly understand preaching in terms of a crisis experience. It is a divine invasion that confronts man with eternal issues and demands decision. The basic presupposition of all Biblical preaching is that man is enslaved to evil. When the Gospel comes, it comes as deliverance. In the proclamation man is personally addressed by the eternal Word of God. He is offered deliverance.

9 Stewart, *A Faith to Proclaim*, p. 43.

10 "Es ist schliesslich nicht der Pfarrer, der verkündigt, sondern *Gott*, der Vater, der Sohn und der Heilige Geist, wirkt durch ihn." (Bo Reicke, "Das Kerygma des Neuen Testaments," *Verhandlungen des schweizerischen reformierten Pfarrvereins*, 89. *Versammlung*, p. 63).

11 C. K. Barrett, *Biblical Preaching and Biblical Scholarship*, p. 4.

12 Gustaf Wingren, *Predikan; en principiell studie*, p. 296, cited by E. Jerome Johanson, *Theology Today*, VIII (Oct. 1951), 356. Johanson's article ("What It Means to Preach the Gospel") is a detailed review of Wingren's book (written in Swedish) on the fundamental character of Christian preaching.

God speaks: man must respond. The demand for decision is inescapable.

Finally, we have come to realize that the ultimate test of the genuineness of preaching is, Does it really convey the saving action of God? A sermon may be true, interesting, and even vitally important, but unless something actually takes place, it is not preaching. True preaching is an event — an event that effectively communicates the power and redemptive activity of God.

This, then, is preaching — the timeless link between act and response that prolongs and mediates the redemptive activity of God. Wherever preaching is true to its essential nature, this is what takes place.

But now the question arises as to the validity of the *kerygma* for modern preaching. Can we of the twentieth century, with all our cultural sophistication and scientific progress, still proclaim the same Gospel that the first apostles proclaimed? Can we preach the Cross and the Empty Tomb with any confidence that they will be relevant to the needs of modern man, or must we exchange these ancient truths for a more up-to-date message, such as the irrepressible spirituality of human nature?

This was the fateful decision of nineteenth-century Liberalism. Enamored by his own progress, man began to redefine the Gospel in terms of what he could do, rather than what God had done. The kerygmatic emphasis upon the death and resurrection of Jesus was ultimately vaporized in humanistic optimism. We need not, however, at this point enter into a critique of Liberalism. Little can be added to what history has already disclosed of its moral impotence. Any philosophy that refuses to grapple with the basic issues of human existence need not expect longevity.

It should be noted in passing that much modern talk about the necessity for relevant preaching misses the mark because it interprets relevancy as no more than a sort of friendly rapport with the spirit of the age. It deals with the Gospel and man's culture, not the Gospel and man's need. Its concept of what makes preaching relevant lies much too close to the surface of things. Just because a sermon is couched in the latest idiom and addressed to a contemporary situation does not make it truly relevant. To be genuinely relevant it must be addressed to man's ultimate spiritual need. It must deal with those questions that lie at the heart of human existence. It must answer man's predicament. It must deal with sin and offer salvation. Only the preaching of the Gospel is preaching that is truly relevant. Any particular sermon is relevant only to the degree that it sets forth what God has done for man's basic and agelong need. John Knox has rightly said, "Only authentically biblical preaching can be really relevant; only vitally relevant preaching can be really biblical."[13]

The real answer to the question of the relevancy of the *kerygma* is found in our new understanding of the essential nature of preaching. If preaching be the extension in time of God's great redemptive act, then not only *may* we preach the *kerygma* today, but we *must*. Nothing else is truly relevant. If the redemptive Self-disclosure of God in Christ Jesus (centering in His death, resurrection, and exaltation) be not proclaimed — re-enacted in a great "I-Thou" encounter — how then can God redeem? It is through the "foolishness of preaching" that God saves those who believe. The *kerygma* is the unique and divinely ordained medium for conveying this saving activity of God. Although rooted in the past, it can be experienced only in the present. As long as man is by nature enslaved to evil, so long will the *kerygma* be vitally relevant to his greatest need.

A closely related problem is that of communication — how effectively to transmit this ancient account of divine intervention to modern man. That the *kerygma* must always be proclaimed in the language of the hearer is an obvious truth. "If the Church of the twentieth century is bound in its utterance by the cadences of seventeenth-century prose and nineteenth-century poetry it is not surprising that it is an opaque medium for the Word of God."[14] Only by being completely modern can it be completely true to itself. The precedent was set when, within the bounds of the New Testament itself, writers like John and the author of Hebrews restated Biblical con-

---

13 Knox, *op. cit.*, p. 27.
14 David H. C. Read, *The Communication of the Gospel*, p. 71.

cepts in terms that were meaningful to their ever-widening audience.

While the need for modernization is always present, it is felt that many modern treatments of the breakdown of religious communication have somewhat overstated the problem. Hendrik Kraemer, for example, writes that the Bible is "unintelligible," the *kerygma* "incomprehensible," and the great key ideas of the Christian faith are "undecipherable hieroglyphs."[15] This can hardly be. As Stewart pointedly says, "Much of the talk one hears about the incomprehensibleness of the vocabulary of religion to the man in the street is . . . a slur upon the average man's intelligence."[16] All such approaches to the problem of communication invariably issue in a plea for the translation of archaic terminology and the modernization of antiquated modes of thought.[17]

With this crusade for linguistic renovation we are in perfect agreement — that is, as long as such modernization actually clarifies the basic message and does not subtly turn it into something that it was never meant to be. What we do not agree with is that, once the renovation is complete, the problem of communication is thereby solved.

The real problem does not lie in the sphere of semantics. It goes much deeper. The failure of the Gospel to be communicated is basically due to man's unwillingness to hear, not to his inability to understand. It is not so much a question of not being able to understand as it is of not wanting to understand. God speaks, but man stuffs his fingers into his ears. At bottom, communication is a theological problem. While we must do everything within our power to proclaim the message of divine deliverance with utmost clarity, the effective communication of that message is, ultimately, the work of God Himself. This does not lessen the responsibility of the preacher. On the contrary, it lays upon him the burden of so being

15 Hendrik Kraemer, *The Communication of the Christian Faith*, pp. 93, 110, 94.

16 Stewart, *A Faith to Proclaim*, p. 44.

17 Bultmann's school of "demythologizing" is the outstanding example of the latter.

taken up into his message that his proclamation of the Gospel becomes a part of that Gospel — a medium for the ongoing redemptive activity of God.

To proclaim the message of divine deliverance is the most solemn responsibility ever entrusted to mortal man. When the preacher mounts the pulpit steps he does so under obligation to mediate the presence of Almighty God. He is not there to air his own views or to hold up a mirror to the times. It is not even enough that he should speak *about* God; he must allow *God* to speak. His words must bear the Divine Word. His voice must be God's voice. He stands before a group of people whose one great need is to be ushered into the presence of God. If his pulpit has become no more than a platform for religious propaganda, he may either interest or bore his people, depending upon his innate ability, but he will never discharge his sacred obligation to mediate the Divine Presence.

This is a matter of awesome significance because it involves the eternal destiny of mankind. If God, in redeeming power, be not present in the proclamation of the Gospel, man will be swept on into an eternity without God and without hope. Apart from an encounter, there can be no salvation. Apart from preaching (interpreted in its widest sense as the effective communication of the Gospel — either oral or written), there can be no redemptive encounter. The fearful responsibility of the Christian herald is so to proclaim the Gospel that "The Miracle" takes place — God is there confronting men in judgment and offering divine deliverance. To fail in this crucial obligation is to betray both God and man.

Who then dares to preach? Who is it that will knowingly assume such responsibility? Only those who have been commissioned by God — those who are compelled to cry out with Jeremiah, "There is in my heart as it were a burning fire shut up in my bones, and I am weary with holding it in, and I cannot" (Jer. 20:9). Without this divine compulsion there can be no effective communication. While there may be an impartation of religious ideas, there will be no real preaching. God will not be there in saving action. Only when a man can say,

"Woe to me if I do not preach the gospel!" (I Cor. 9:16) will his awkward and stumbling words become the voice of God.

But preaching is more than obligation only. The measure of responsibility is also the measure of privilege. The commission to preach, while a solemn trust, is also the greatest honor that can be bestowed upon a man. What other calling elevates man to the role of co-worker with God in the impartation of eternal salvation? Who else can open his mouth and speak, knowing that his words will somehow convey the Divine Word? It has fallen to the preacher to mediate the saving action of God. He is a priest whose message is the sacrament of salvation. As he by faith proclaims the great Act of God, he realizes that it is once again taking place. The Cross becomes a present reality. God is revealing Himself through Christ Jesus. Man is offered deliverance and moved to respond in faith. Without preaching, salvation would be theory only. It is the inestimable privilege of the preacher to prolong in time that one great Act which alone gives meaning to time.

Let us, then, have men who have grasped the significance of their high calling — men who are possessed with the urgency of the Gospel. Let us have men who, like the apostle Paul, "tremble" lest their speech and message be not a demonstration of the Spirit and power (I Cor. 2:3-4). "When all is said and done," writes J. S. Stewart, "the supreme need of the Church . . . is men on fire for Christ"[18] — men who in the truest sense of the word are heralds of God.

18 Stewart, *Heralds of God*, p. 220.

INDEX OF AUTHORS

INDEX OF SUBJECTS

INDEX OF SCRIPTURE PASSAGES

INDEX OF NON-BIBLICAL REFERENCES